From My Window

The Diary
of
Althea Fanshawe

of
13 Brock Street,
Bath

From My Window

The Diary of Althea Fanshawe

of
13 Brock Street,
Bath

Transcribed and researched
by Deirdre Marculescu

Valence House Publications

Published in 2025 by Valence House Publications
Valence House, Becontree Avenue
Dagenham, Essex RM8 3HT

www.valencehousecollections.co.uk

ISBN 978-1-911391-13-5

Introduction and all editorial material copyright ©Valence House Publications 2025

All rights reserved. No part of this book may be reproduced or transmitted in any form or by any means, electronic or mechanical, including photocopying, recording or by any information storage or retrieval system, without permission from the Publisher in writing

Previous Fanshawe Publications
Sebastopol to Dagenham (978-1-911391-02-9)
Abyssinia 1868 (978-1-911391-04-3)
Fanshawe's Indian Summer (978-1-911391-05-0)
Parsloes to Pompeii (978-1-911391-10-4)
The Life of Sir Richard Fanshawe (978-1-911391-00-5)

Cover Images :
Cover of Althea Fanshawe's diary (Original) and image of Althea Fanshawe's bookplate - Local Studies and Archives at Valence House Museum
Mrs Graham's Hot Air Balloon - Wikicommons
19th Century map of Bath by John Rapkin, 1851

Contents

Althea's Life & family　　　　　　　Pages i - xxvii

Custodians of the Diary　　　　　　Page xxviii

Transcriber's notes　　　　　　　　Pages xxix - xxx

Diary　　　　　　　　　　　　　　Pages 1 - 200

Letters from Custodians　　　　　　Pages 201 - 202

Appendix 1
**Henry Fanshawe of Dengie & Martin
(Extract from
The History of The Fanshawe Family)**　　Pages 203 - 213

Appendix 2
Caleb Hillier Parry (1755-1822)　　　Pages 214 - 223

Appendix 3
**From Manuscript to Print – 1829
(The Memoirs of Ann, Lady Fanshawe)**　　Pages 224 - 233

Illustrations and Acknowledgments　　Pages 234 – 235

Historical Resources for Further Reading　Pages 236 - 237

Althea's Life & family

Bath with elegant terraces and crescents, had become well established by the beginning of the 19th century and enjoyed the patronage of royalty. Then after some years of first attracting fashionable visitors with its spa waters and public assemblies, the city gradually became home to a more aged elite society.

These permanent residents of Bath possibly appreciated an atmosphere more at ease than in London, where they found congenial neighbours and friends who offered a gentler society. Perhaps too, for the elderly and sick, there was comfort in having close at hand the established practices of some of the best doctors in the country.

When Althea Fanshawe and her mother settled permanently at Bath during 1803 the city was already familiar to them as they had been resident when Althea's father died in 1777 and was buried in the Abbey. However, the main home of the family since 1760 was always at Shiplake, near Henley-on-Thames, situated on the banks of a beautiful part of that river.

Then as now, Henley was celebrated for delightful river activities and festivals, enjoyed mostly by those privileged in society and in consequence, Althea's family were part of a comfortable circle of friends and neighbours with shared mutual friendship and many interests. These were happy memories for Althea and many entries in her diary reflect those connections.

Surely then it must have been difficult for Althea to leave such pleasant living conditions and memories, but perhaps it was with an awareness of increasing health problems at the age of forty-three that she planned with her elderly mother, for the time when she would live alone.

Althea began her diary in 1805 by confirming that her mother had died in January that year. Then by qualifying the exact purpose of the record she was intending to keep; she made clear it was entirely for her own personal record and reference which is why she did not include any 'unnecessary' explanations. But today, we are strangers to her world and to complete those gaps we need to understand what she considered important, how she fitted into her family and her position in society.

Family life

Althea Fanshawe was born at Savile Row, Westminster on 11th February 1759 when her father Simon Fanshawe was MP for Grampond[1] and Comptroller of the Household of the Prince of Wales. He was married in 1753 to his first cousin Althea Snelling, when he was thirty-seven and she only twenty-three. Their first child called Althea was born within a year and their only son, Henry followed in 1756. Then the next year, little Althea died so when a second daughter arrived in 1759, she also was given the name Althea. Then to complete the family, another daughter was born in 1760 and named Frances.

Althea's family were from the class recognised as 'the gentry' with her father tracing his ancestry directly back to Fanshawe Gate - a property situated on Derbyshire's northern border that from medieval times had been passed from father to eldest son, or the next male in the family pedigree. However, Althea inherited Fanshawe Gate - a departure from tradition explained by specific instructions left by her father that the property must not be passed to his only son. His reasons will soon become clear, but as we know Althea ultimately had that responsibility, we can observe how seriously she viewed that obligation through the entries in her diary.

Althea's ancestors first rose to historical prominence after Henry Fanshawe entered the Tudor court as a clerk in the Office of the Remembrancer of the Exchequer in 1522. Many years later when appointed Queen Elizabeth's Remembrancer, he also obtained the reversion of the position, enabling his nephew and prodigy Thomas Fanshawe to succeed in 1568.

Already a proven and trusted administrator, Queen Elizabeth's appointed 2nd Remembrancer became a close confidante

---

[1] a former Cornish constituency.

of Lord Burghley and established many other important connections through the course of his public duties. Among whom were the City magnates of the great livery companies which lead to his children making suitable and successful marriages into those powerful families. Through his reputation and abilities, his male descendants were able to continue to exercise the family's right of reversion for the post of Remembrancer long after his death and he left his family financially secure with considerable land and property holdings in Dagenham and Barking, together with the large estate of Ware Park on the Great North Road. His estate was fairly divided between his three sons who through their descendants form the lineage that has claim to that most important part of Fanshawe history.

Secure in positions within the court of Charles I, the family entered the Civil War and all declared loyalty to the King. They were ultimately to suffer the consequences of that loyalty but perhaps as some recompense, Ware Park's eldest son was made a viscount, and his brothers received knighthoods (most notably, Sir Richard Fanshawe, later Charles II's first Ambassador to Spain).

Unfortunately, by funding loyal support and settling compound fines to the Republicans, the loss of Ware Park resulted. Sadly too, their titles were all extinct within a few generations - the title of the 3rd Remembrancer's elder son, Viscount Dromore extinct in 1716, and that of the second son Sir Thomas Fanshawe of Jenkins in 1705. Consequently, only the male descendants of the third son, William Fanshawe of Parsloes remains to carry the family name and lineage back to Thomas Fanshawe the 2nd Remembrancer.

Fortunately, that line is strong and survives through two separate strands. The 'senior' line, called the Dengie branch are the direct descendants of Althea's great-grandfather, William Fanshawe who died in 1708, but he did not inherit the Parsloes estate although the eldest son – the result of a dispute with his father, partly by religion but more probably his choice of wife[1].

---

[1] Mary Walters - daughter of Lucy Walters, an early mistress of King Charles II and the mother of James, Duke of Monmouth, recognised by the King as his eldest son.

Consequently, John Fanshawe, his younger half-brother inherited the Parsloes estate, so it is his descendants who are known as the Parsloes line – with the estate remaining in the family until the beginning of the 20th century.

Despite this loss of inheritance, the seniority of Althea's ancestor William Fanshawe was never in dispute where the old family property of Fanshawe Gate was concerned. This was recognised by the last male of the Ware Park line - Simon Fanshawe, 5th Viscount Dromore for when he died, Althea's father became the most senior direct male descendants of Thomas Fanshawe 2nd Remembrancer.

This demonstrates how and the purpose of the three branches of the Fanshawe family remaining in touch through several centuries. Through Althea's diary, we can observe her interest in distant 'Parsloes' cousins when she records entertaining the three daughters of John Fanshawe of Shabden just before they left England to travel in Europe. These three ladies were all artistically gifted but the most known and independent was the published poetess Catherine Maria Fanshawe and her original sketchbook from her journey through Italy, is now preserved in the Fanshawe Collection at Valence House.

Clearly the three sisters appreciated their links to their 'Dengie' cousins, but perhaps they had a special interested as Althea's father had helped their own father into his first position as a clerk to the Board of the Green Cloth. Subsequently he became Receiver of Fines in the Lord Chancellor's Office.

With this demonstration of how important family connections were to gentry families we can appreciate that by helping each other all re-established their place in society. This kept alive the possibility of professional and marriage ambitions and allows us to appreciate how each gentleman's wife brought her own important connections into the Fanshawe circle.

William Fanshawe of Parsloes (1583 - 1634)
3rd son of Thomas Fanshawe 2nd Remembrancer
Valence House (LDVAL45)

Simon Fanshawe of Fanshawe Gate (1716 - 1777)
Comptroller of the household of the Prince of Wales.
Valence House (LDVAL 2019.1.4)

The Snelling Family

Althea's story could not be complete without the history of the Snelling family as both her father and grandfather married into the same family.

The Snellings, originally from Suffolk, were by the 17th century very wealthy merchants as William Snelling, Althea's great-grandfather, was a member of The Levant Company. Formed in 1581, that company had been granted a trading monopoly with the Ottoman Empire by a Royal Charter from Queen Elizabeth and whilst these great trading companies kept open political channels between nation states, the traders had advantageous access to the flow of goods from the East.

The centre for the Levant Company was Aleppo[1] - a large cosmopolitan city full of ambitious men handling vital luxury commodities such as furs, silk, spices, raisins and currents. However, although similar to all trading there was financial risk, in Aleppo there was the additional hazard of disease and epidemics which thrived in such a hot and crowded eastern environ.

Fortunately, William Snelling survived to become a substantial merchant and acquired a mansion home in London at Bromley St. Leonards by Bow. When he died in 1712, his property left to his wife, was entailed to be passed after seven years to his son William – also a merchant, in Aleppo at the time of his father's death.

Two years after the elder William Snelling's death, his only daughter Elizabeth Snelling married Thomas Edward Fanshawe who at a similar time was petitioning the Crown for the reversion of the post of King's Remembrancer. Their marriage settlements included her father's legacy of £4,000 and in return, the Fanshawe property of Great Singleton was settled on the bride.

Of the couple's five children, only three survived and of those the only son was Althea's father Simon Fanshawe, born in 1715 who was only ten when his father died. His mother made a

---

[1] Modern day Syria.

second marriage and a half-sister was born with whom he was close and the lady, Elizabeth Hozier is mentioned by Althea in the diary.

We must assume 'the Snellings' became important in Simon Fanshawe's young life after the death of his father. When later his mother's brother William Snelling married Anna Hyde in 1724, he came to acquire two young cousins Anna born in 1726, and her sister Althea in 1730. Then perhaps, when his uncle the younger William Snelling died in 1738, Simon Fanshawe at the age of twenty-three was obliged to take an interest in the welfare of those two young girls?

Little is really known of Simon Fanshawe until his election to the House of Commons. No evidence has been found of his attendance at formal school or university, yet he was well-educated. Probably he was tutored at home by a cleric or boarded at a tutor-cleric's vicarage. He may also have travelled in Europe with a tutor but there is nothing to confirm. However, of his character, the mature Simon Fanshawe seen in his portrait at Valence House Museum, appears to be a gentleman with an amiable disposition displayed by the artist as confident and relaxed as if in conversation.

The painter William Hoare was well-used to elite clients as he had been the first to set up a studio in Bath; recognising the quality of the residents of the city. Possibly he was a little generous regarding this sitter's weight, or perhaps Lord Waldegrave was a little unkind when in 1756 he wrote Simon Fanshawe's recommendation for a Royal Household position: *'I shall certainly not think of recommending him as a groom of the bedchamber, and he exceeds the weight of an equerry by at least ten stone. But he is a very proper person to keep his Royal Highness's cooks under good discipline, to speak with authority to purveyors, wine merchants, cellar men etc., and consequently well qualified to be a clerk of the Green Cloth…can recommend him as a gentleman who may be depended on, whose conduct in Parliament has even been clear and uniform, of whom Mr Pelham had a thorough good opinion, and who I know both in his private and political capacity, to be an honest man and a man of honour…'* however, the artist was a protégé of Pelham and Simon Fanshawe was in the parliamentary group that gathered around Pelham (Duke of Newcastle).

As we know, Simon Fanshawe married his younger cousin Althea Snelling and each was comfortably and independently positioned to live well. Their close family marriage brought together the almost undiluted legacies of at least two generations of wealthy Snelling merchants and by 1760 they acquired a lease on a country house at Shiplake, whilst maintaining a town house in Savile Row.

In the publication 'The History of the Fanshawe Family' prepared in the early 20th century, the name of their property at Shiplake is given as 'Whitehouse' with the author, citing his source of reference as a 'Mrs Climenson'. However, this fact is contradicted by information in the letters and diaries, contemporary to the 18th century written by Mrs Philip Lybbe Powys of Hardwick House and Fawley Rectory at Henley.

From 1756 until her death in 1808, Mrs Lybbe Powys kept very detailed accounts of her travels whilst also sharing through her journals the activities of her home neighbourhood - and curiously, the same 'Emily Climenson' edited those papers, published in 1899.

Those journals give access to the life enjoyed at Shiplake by a circle of neighbourhood friends including Althea's mother, Mrs Althea Fanshawe. Those journals have proved extremely useful in identifying the many friends and neighbours to whom Althea refers in her diary and whilst keeping that in mind, note the following entry by Mrs Lybbe Powys in 1788 …'*19th October – On Friday began our Winter Henley ball, and was a very full one, the whole neighbouring families making it a point to attend. Got home about four, as there is always a supper and dancing after. We were gay this autumn, having a very tolerable set of strollers at Henley; most of the ladies bespoke plays, as Lady Ailesbury, Mrs Damer, both Mrs Freeman, Mrs Fanshawe, Miss Grote myself etc, we had all the families attended each other's nights, we had very crowded houses, which lasted all that moon.'*

That entry is particularly interesting as despite Mrs Fanshawe being mentioned several times in the journals of Mrs Lybbe Powys, only in this context has Emily Climenson the transposer, indicated this reference against her name … *'living at Holmwood, Shiplake'*.

It is probable that the house occupied by the Fanshawe family was not the one called 'White House' for although it was/is a substantial house, it appears to have been built in the early 20th century. Perhaps a house existed previously with the same name on that site which might have been the property Simon Fanshawe leased first. However, the house named 'Holmwood' has a more certain history having been built early in the 18th century as a typical Georgian gentleman's residence. Today, the same house, much restored and updated exists, and if it should interest was recently home to Rupert Murdoch.

More certain, is the fact that Simon Fanshawe did not stand for re-election to parliament after 1768, having the year previously resigned his post as Comptroller of the Board of the Green Cloth for which he was in receipt of a secret service pension of £800. Consequently, at the age of fifty-two and having considerable means, he effectively retired from public life. He died in January 1777 so perhaps it is safe to imagine he spent the intervening years moving pleasantly between Shiplake, London and Bath – with only a concern for his son's profligate waste of money to disrupt his retirement?

'My Brother'

Althea's brother Henry was educated at Eton, and in 1770 gazetted into 1st Foot Guards. Within two years, commissions were purchased by his father at a cost of £1,500 enabling him to arrive at the rank of adjutant, attached to the company of his cousin, Colonel West Hyde. After his father's death, another investment of £5,000 was made to secure his captaincy but unfortunately, soon all his commissions were sold to settle debts caused entirely to his personal financial recklessness. Consequently, his resignation was forced by his Regiment.

Despite his marriage to Susanna Le Grys, an heiress to a considerable fortune, he was in an acute financial situation as adding to the debt he had to support four children who arrived in quick succession. Although, able to transfer to the 83rd Regiment as Lt. Colonel, even that commission had to be sold very soon after. By 1783 he was unemployed and forced to take his family abroad in an attempt to live more simply.

Eventually his fortune turned with the help of General Conway[1] of Park Place, Henley - a family friend and neighbour, well-known for his kindness who had already assisted Henry with the sale of his commissions. Next, he agreed to appeal to King George III on his behalf, which resulted in the King insisting that Henry Fanshawe must remain prohibited from ever serving in any of his regiments. However, permission was gained for him to enlist in the army of a British ally, carrying with him the rank of Colonel.

Obviously, Althea's father had anticipated his son's finances would become a problem and writing his will, he took that into account. Whilst not excluding Henry as a beneficiary, he insured his access was restricted and similarly, with that lack of confidence, he caused Fanshawe Gate not to be passed to his only son - instead, the property was left to his widow to pass to Althea.

With this brief explanation, a reader's initial queries concerning why Henry Fanshawe went to Russia to become a General and a Senator are answered and his unusual life story as described through Althea's diary, may be understood. A fuller account[2] of his achievements in the Imperial Russian Army and those of his sons is contained in 'The History of the Fanshawe Family'- the recognised invaluable family resource produced by one of his many descendants, Herbert C Fanshawe.

---

[1] Field Marshall Henry Seymour Conway (1721-1795), cousin of Horace Walpole and brother of 1st Marquis of Hertford.
[2] See Appendix 1.

It is important to mention here that Althea's diary originally provided HCF with the first broad outline of his great-grandfather's activities. Later he expanded the story through his own research, but in the original of the diary he left his marks and comments against the events he wished to highlight. He also compiled his own index on the unused final pages of the diary – demonstrating his efforts as initially he tried to get to grips with that vast expanse of military action.

'My Sister'

In Althea's time, young gentlemen were often attracted to military and naval careers due to the scope for advancement of status as well as the possibility of adventure and distant travel. So, finding Althea's sister, Frances had married a military man, is not surprising.

In 1782, when Althea and Frances visited their brother Henry stationed with his regiment on the island of Guernsey, also there was Captain John Jenkinson with the 95th Regiment. This soldier who enjoyed a long career, reached the rank of Lieutenant General by 1821 when appointed Inspecting Officer of the Volunteers. However, in the earlier years of the diary, we learn of Frances travelling with her husband and family through France, and how after a long separation, she and her brother Henry could meet and bring their families together.

John and Frances Jenkinson, with seven daughters and four sons suffered tragic loss – sons died through military action and daughters, who died young and unexpectedly from epidemic diseases, whilst in France. As Althea records the deaths of those young nephews and nieces, her entries appear dispassionate but surely masked her very personal sorrow. We can catch rare glimpses of Althea's feelings and intuition from unusual comments in her diary concerning the health of her eldest niece, Fanny. Her fears for her niece's mental health were proven correct many years after her own death - as public records reveal that in later life, Fanny lived as a privately funded in-patient of Brislington House, a 'modern' lunatic asylum. Presumably, a need for special care was anticipated by her father, when he left funding through a special legacy.

Unfortunately, Althea's diary does not 'paint' the character of her sister Frances Jenkinson very strongly, but she has the potential to be particularly interesting. By repute she kept a diary *'all her life'* and it is recorded that early in the 20th century her diaries were kept by her granddaughter Mrs Mary Jebb. Hopefully they are still treasured by her descendants and perhaps one day another fascinating life story will be revealed.

The Diary

Thinking now of Althea's Diary – this small notebook diary together with her published books, are all that speak for Althea's personality and character, so it is fortunate that along with other family documents, Althea's Diary has been carefully stored by succeeding senior members of the Dengie branch of the family.

Always aware of the importance of their story, more recently the family's concern grew for the long-term safekeeping of their archive. Fortunately, they were aware that since the 1960's the London Borough of Barking & Dagenham has been the privileged custodians of the main 'Fanshawe Collection' and by approaching Valence House Museum & Local Studies Centre where the collection is stored, they gained a very positive response.

As soon as the Dengie family archive was received into the collection, work quickly began on the catalogue. Althea's Diary, already known as possibly significant, it became a priority to make a transcription that would allow the contents to be more easily read and researched. Although it was known that extracts had been used during the preparation of 'The History of the Fanshawe Family', the contents overall and their relevance had not previously been established. However, with the diary transposed and the entries fully researched, we can assert with confidence that Althea Fanshawe's profile must urgently be re-considered. Her personality must be brought into the light so that she is viewed as among the more interesting characters of the Fanshawe family.

Althea Fanshawe was obviously a very practical woman for when she identified her need to keep a diary, she succinctly clarified the purpose it should serve, organising it with competence to enable quick reference. By making her statement of purpose on the opening page, she confirms serious intent and by drawing up the pages, she opened the first year using her methodical mind to divide her records by subjects and interest. With that arrangement working so well, she continued without variance throughout the years – her only possible exception may have been the addition of her reference index, located on the final pages of the original. Her entries were made timely and without interruption, although, in the last years, some may have been slightly retrospective. They only ceased when she became seriously ill during February 1824 - a few weeks before her death.

Unlike her sister Frances, this diary seems to be the only period Althea maintained this type of record as from her own comments, it must be assumed that whilst she lived at home with her mother, she relied on a diary reputedly kept by Mrs Fanshawe.

Althea would not have been fazed by the prospect of writing. By 1805 she had written two books and a further three were written during the period of the diary - all with considerable critical success. Yet as most potential diarists discover, the rigor needed to make regular entries requires a determined talent, especially if public events are to be included, as they need be relative, selective and of more than immediate local interest.

Whilst most people never attempt to write a book, almost all who are literate try to keep a diary for a short while. They take many forms, from child-like to extremely sophisticated but most are relatively short and usually become lost. If they survive, included will often be a few lines telling of major events, viewed within context and place, hidden amid much personal information. It is for this reason that along with professional journalists, a diarist's words stand as important as those of writers of private letters as each gives a unique view, unedited by time, as opposed to a memoirist whose reflective thoughts may be distorted.

Althea wrote directly from thought to hand and her information was rarely corrected which leaves her opinions and ideas free to be challenged later - either by herself or another reader. That fact alone makes a diary interesting and fascinating, and any transcriber must endeavour to ensure all words remain unchanged from the original. If this has been achieved with Althea's diary, then her honest views surely deserve comparison with those of her contemporaries.

Whilst that is true, the transposer's thoughts will inevitably be coloured by what is revealed and naturally, assessments will be made about the subject's life, character and interests. Another reader of Althea's diary may form different views, but I am certain that most readers will quickly build an image of Althea Fanshawe.

Until now, all that is really known of Althea has been gleaned from the few lines within the 'The History of the Fanshawe Family'. So, without bias, we should keep in mind that the author HCF was male, a relative and of another generation to Althea – and of us today! He created a sympathetic record of her life from having 'read' the diary but used the contents only to assemble facts about the activities of others in her family, particularly her brother Henry, his own ancestor. Unfortunately, or maybe fortunately - he left his comments in the diary whilst it was in his possession, so we must assume he did not appreciate the diary as a valuable archival document but used it in the same way as the many published historical works in his library[1], which he marked similarly.

From HCF's point of view, the impression is given that Althea's published writing was a little trivial and in November 1915, he records within the original diary the opinions of the three lady cousins of Shabden, given after visiting Althea ... *Miss Penelope*

---

[1] H C Fanshawe's library now included in the Fanshawe Collection at Valence House – was used to assist him in his monumental task of producing a family history in 535 pages. Most of these antiquarian books were marked and indexed.

Fanshawe recorded in her journal of November 1816 that she visited Miss Althea Fanshawe frequently 'a sad monument of the afflicting this not destructive (!) effects of epilepsy. She has been for 22 years a confirmed invalid, seeing but few relations & Mr & Mrs Bowdler. Considering the life she leads it is astonishing that her faculties are not more impaired for she is able to employ all her time reading, writing and work. Her chief defect is from want of communication with others, which throws her back entirely upon herself & her few concerns & renders her open to such prejudices & too little able to vary her source of ideas with what is passing around her'…

Whatever was his own view, HCF was more subtle in his comments in the family history *'The three sisters visited Miss Althea Fanshawe in Bath in November 1816 and recorded the opinion that she was a wonderful person for one so cruelly afflicted by constant fits of epilepsy'*…

Unfortunately, because of those statements, the true strength of Althea Fanshawe's character has since been buried - but now we have the opportunity to re-evaluate her life and work, especially since more recently her profile has been 'picked up' by some 'feminist' literary writers.

That said, we must be cautious for after many decades we may think we are able to evaluate female independence easily but it must be acknowledge that Althea seems to have been of the persuasion that women could achieve their ambitions in many ways - not necessarily those that would attract her to modern feminist causes.

Perhaps we should begin by clarifying Althea's single status, for as a woman of her class with financial security, her choices were more than most. Yet, as a victim of a very debilitating illness, her ability to travel was restricted, and curtailed most of her active life. However, we should not ignore the fact that apparently, she was about thirty before experiencing signs of epilepsy.

The established view has always been that she suffered from epilepsy but notably in the diary she does not give a name to her illness - however she reveals the name of her doctor on the opening pages.

By 1805, Dr Caleb Hillier Parry was so well-established at Bath - he may have been a reason for Althea moving to the city. Although an eminent doctor, he was obviously unable to offer Althea a cure but no doubt he gave her confidence by sharing his knowledge and friendship. By reputation, he was a particularly kind and entertaining man who took time to talk with his patients but perhaps most interestingly, he was an early 'curious' physician who observed and kept extensive records.

Modern medicine has built upon the foundations laid by the brilliance of Parry and his colleagues - enlightened men who never missed opportunities to learn the workings of the human body. We are fortunate that Parry's copious notes[1] remain to be searched and among his many pages of observations and diagnosis are references to patient 'Miss F'. This lady records her numbers of fits and attacks and in the chart within Parry's notes the numbers tally with those kept by Althea in her diary. There is also further unmistakable identifying information included and also we learn there of her first fit occurring in September 1794.

Without access to modern medication, Althea's life eventually became governed by her 'Epilepsy' and through her diary we observe how her confidence gradually ebbed away until she hardly dared to venture out. Fortunately, her younger life was not so restricted as at twenty-two she travelled to Guernsey with her sister Frances, then after to London to be a witness to her sister's marriage. At some point she made a journey through Europe – confirmed by her diary entry for the death of Louis Tessier in 1811 - *'whom I knew at Naples'*.

While living at Shiplake with her mother they both actively shared the friendly entertainment of their neighbourhood - many of those friends are later recorded in her births, marriages and deaths charts. However, just after the death of their father, her brother

---

[1] See Appendix 2 - Dr Caleb Hillier Parry.

Henry caused such concern by losing his commission in the Guards and his situation as a married man with four young sons created a family crisis. This explains why so much in the diary concerns Henry's responsibilities to all his sons as when joining his new Russian Regiment in Crimea during 1784, he had little choice but to leave his two eldest boys in England. This resulted in the younger boy, Charles Robert, then about four, being placed in the care of Mrs Fanshawe and his Aunt Althea, where he remained all his childhood.

It is evident from the first pages of her diary that Althea had a special relationship with Charles but knowing and loving the young man as a son, she knew that like his father, he was unable to manage money. Whilst recording her nephew's marriage, and the births of his many children, a sense of tension is exposed whenever Charles requests money. This being constant, Althea shared her frustration with her diary, causing her to leave some marks of punctuation against his pleas.

Despite many good opportunities, Revd Charles Fanshawe never became the master of his accounts, but we learn how the Duke and Duchess of Clarence became his royal patrons. Through that connection it becomes possible to trace Althea's contribution to the first publication of the Memoirs of Ann Lady Fanshawe[1] - that edition published in 1829, with Charles Fanshawe's dedication to the Duchess, was based upon the copy made by Althea from an original copy of the manuscript.

Althea's relationship with Charles seems complex - noticeably she never refers to his wife by her first name, yet when Patty suffered a painful and dreadful illness, we can sense Althea's sympathy for the couple was real. Then through the family tragedy of Patty's death, Althea makes Charles the heir to Fanshawe Gate and her personal estate.

---

[1] See Appendix 3 – Ann, Lady Fanshawe.

The wider family

Althea was always very particular in keeping connections with her wider family and possibly because her close family was relatively small and often overseas, she enjoyed having many cousins. By never confusing friends with her family, she kept the two groups clearly separate throughout her diary, making research easier and rewarding.

Until more recent generations, all families considered 'family' in the wider sense and cousins of several degrees kept closely in touch with all viewed as important. The inter-connections of the Fanshawe family are well documented and for reference especially helpful are the pedigrees prepared by Beaujolois Mabel Ridout - a 'Parsloes cousin' known to have assembled them for HCF's 'The History of the Fanshawe Family'.

Not so familiar are the relatives of Althea's mother, Althea Snelling whose parents were William Snelling and his wife Anna Hyde. Therefore, the cousins we will review first are the many children of Anna Hyde's brother John:

The fifth child has already been mentioned - he was West Hyde, the colonel attached to the Regiment of Guards in which Henry Fanshawe first served. More important to Althea was the eighth child, also named Althea and born the same year as her first cousin Althea Snelling (Mrs Fanshawe). Those two girls grew up close and after Althea Hyde's marriage to Revd Francis Wollaston in 1758, her children were among Althea's closest family and friends.

The Rector of Chislehurst from 1761 until 1815, Revd Francis Wollaston was another of those 18th century 'curious' man with scientific interests. With his own observatory he studied astronomy and through his published academic papers was elected a fellow of the Royal Society in 1769.

Among their children (Althea's second cousins) whom she generally calls 'The Wollastons', were some interesting personalities such as William Hyde Wollaston a physiologist, chemist & physicist, and Francis John Hyde Wollaston a philosopher. Other sons became senior clergymen, and all their sisters married well, including Mary Wollaston, the wife of the 'Physician in Ordinary' to King George III - Dr William Heberden, son of another eminent doctor, William Heberden the elder (both doctors were colleagues of Dr Caleb Hillier Parry).

Friends and Acquaintances

Among such educated people we can only imagine the level of conversation and the interesting news passed among the cousins but if we also consider the friends that visited Althea and how they too were connected, it is hard to assume her thoughts would be narrow as she sat alone.

Her writing proves she was not governed by her illness but by the flow of letters, visits and the newspapers she read so avidly. And through her diary she demonstrates a wide interest in the world whilst reflecting the part she played in the political and social life of Georgian Bath.

All her friends had something of interest to share. As an example, any reference to Mr Fane relates to John Fane MP for Oxfordshire (1796 to 1815). Although not a party politician he generally supported Pitt's government while retaining his independence and voted by his principles. Officially, his interests were in agriculture but for Althea, he was a reliable man of character who could be trusted to speak with on family matters. His wife, Lady Elizabeth Parker was one of the two daughters of Thomas Parker, 3rd Earl of Macclesfield, and their son Francis Fane, was the brave and adventurous young naval officer, whose daring exploits Althea briefly captures in her diary.

Althea mentions numerous interesting people – and as all had a story to discover, the research for the diary proved intensely absorbing and often entertaining. It is not possible or intended to explore all those lives here, but any interested reader may use the references supplied to delve deeper, with the assurance that Althea will point towards many directions that will tempt the curiosity!

Yet we cannot leave Althea's friends and acquaintances without speaking of Mrs Philip Lybbe Powys. Althea's references to this lady soon aroused my curiosity and with only a little investigation a treasure trove of this lady's letters and diaries were revealed. Although published in 1899, it would seem they still wait to be widely known.

Mrs Philip Lybbe Powys and her husband and family lived at Hardwick House but later moved into Fawley Rectory with her husband's brother, Revd. Thomas Powys. Her writing shares the activities of her community of mutual friends including the Fanshawes, leaving a vivid picture of Shiplake and Henley in the late 18th century.

The Fanshawe & Powys families are further linked - for after the death of Rector Powys in 1810, he was succeeded by his nephew Thomas Powys then when he died in 1817 it was Althea's nephew, Revd Charles Fanshawe who applied to the wealthy Freeman family of Fawley Court and secured that much sought after living.

Mrs Lybbe Powys described Fawley Rectory in 1771 as… *'one of the most elegant parsonages in England, commanding from a very good house a prospect uncommonly noble'*… That newly built house was then occupied by the bachelor rector, Thomas Powys and his boarding pupil, John Pratt. This student remained from the age of nine until going to Cambridge where he became a lifelong friend of William Pitt, the Younger. After inheriting his father's title, as Lord Camden, he then served in Pitt's government, as Lord Lieutenant of Ireland.

This is mentioned merely to demonstrate how men educated privately by a good tutor, often kept that tutor close. Camden and Pitt were both educated in this way, and keeping their tutors as mentors as they progressed, the tutors also gained promotion – Thomas Powys became Dean of Canterbury and Pitt's tutor Edward Wilson, a Canon of Windsor.

Through Mrs Lybbe Powys' diaries we learn much about these pupil/tutor relationships as a form of education which often advantaged gifted and studious boys. There was obviously a financial gain for the clergymen, but through Althea's diary we can also see how royal patronage granted to Charles Fanshawe began when he taught his patron's son. Thus, indicating that the potential for future advantages was perhaps more important than immediate additional income.

Mrs Lybbe Powys provides many such illustrations of 18th century life which helps colour our imagery when we read Althea's chronicles – for as she links their many mutual friends, the 'shorthand' of Althea's aide-memoire is often clarified.

Daily Living

Althea lived from 1805 without a companion of her own status although obviously she kept several servants. Yet the nature of her illness would have required a trusted servant/companion on hand for her safety in the event of seizure. Understandably, Althea chose not to record that aspect of her life and only on April 1st 1811 does she specifically mention help …*Seized with a fit in the Crescent, carried by Dr Bowen into Mrs Gwynne's house & then brought home in a chair*… which must relate to Apothecary Bowen, whose marriage she recorded in 1810.

The diary mentions only two servants - the *death of my ever-lamented Browne* in August 1809 and the recorded death and burial entry in 1815 regarding Jane Sayers, described by Althea with affectionate remembrance, as an old servant of her mother.

However, Althea had many friends and according to her own comments, the Bowdler family were her closest friends in Bath.

Bookplate – Henrietta Maria Bowdler

The personalities of this family are known although Althea's references to Mrs Bowdler are confusing. Clarification only comes through a diary entry in December 1810 …*Miss Bowdler, niece to my friend Mrs H Bowdler*… as this 'Mrs' Bowdler, generally addressed by that title, was not married. All references to 'Mr & Mrs Bowdler' relate correctly to Henrietta Bowdler (1750 - 1830) and her brother Thomas Bowdler (1754 – 1825).

Both the 'Bowdlers' were seriously occupied with writing, so it is very unlikely they enhanced the practicalities of Althea's life but more probably, they were the good friends who provided regular general support. They would also have been a stimulus to Althea's writing ambitions and by keeping up her sense of purpose and her level of personal satisfaction they surely were important to her survival in isolation.

Education and Writing

By acknowledging Althea's motivation during her long and stressful illness, we must now carefully consider her work. Nothing is known of her education, but prior to her brother Henry going to Eton in 1766, preparatory education at home must have taken place. Perhaps then the same tutor or governess also taught Althea and her sister Francis and once Henry moved on, a lady governess was appointed?

The education of Fanshawe ladies was rarely neglected and evidence of a 'superior' education runs though Althea's writing. The confidence and fluency of language in Althea's written work prove that her legacy as a writer need not rest entirely on an interesting and well written diary.

Her published stories and essays deserve appreciation as entertaining and thought-provoking messages aimed at self-improvement and delivered in a style that does not lack humour. They are obviously the outpouring of an enquiring mind which had studied and analysed complex aspects of human nature.

So, as we think about her work, we can imagine her frustration at living isolated at home whilst people were gathering nearby at 16 Royal Crescent to share intellectual interests and ideas at The Blue Stocking Society[1], the centre of enlightened thinking. Often overshadowed by the City's reputation for public assemblies

---

[1] At the home of the founder Elizabeth Montagu.

and romance, the society had formed and met there since the middle of the 18th century where ladies who had grown tired of endless card parties found an intellectual exchange of ideas as they gathered without formality. They were thinkers, writers, artists and poets who actively encouraging men to attend, often as speakers; all fostering the Society's aim to improve women and children's education.

By the early 19th century, formal membership had dwindled due mainly to the deaths of founder members, but still like-minded ladies met in small groups and progressing the Society's aims - and their efforts began the creation of the many opportunities which women cherish and expect today.

Awareness of Althea's historical location provides us with a sense of her interest in the many 'women's issues' in her diary. We will not call her or the ladies she followed 'feminists' for that is a word which limits and over-simplifies their interests and the nature of equality for which they strived. Yet Althea's interest was clearly drawn to ladies with many aims and ambitions.

Important among them was Mrs Sarah Trimmer who was born in 1741 and as noted by Althea in her diary – *'died December 1810'*. Although not a known member of the Blue Stocking Society, Mrs Trimmer was a prime mover in children's education.

When Althea received a letter from Mrs Trimmer in 1809 - she describes it as 'a *most complemental letter*', after a copy of her 'Thoughts on Affectation' had been sent by the publisher - certainly, Althea considered that letter 'an accolade'.

Today, Mrs Trimmer is considered to have been the first to write especially for children. Her 'Fabulous Histories' remained in print for more than a century and all her books were much copied by others, especially those writing animal stories for children. She was also a philanthropist, establishing several Sunday and charity schools and by publishing manuals and textbooks she shared her ideas with others so they too could set up schools. Mrs Trimmer was an enterprising lady who must surely be commended by all -

especially for her idea of presenting characters in the image of animals, for who hasn't fond memories of a favourite animal character encountered when first learning to read?

Another lady of a different character noted by Althea was Hester Thrale (1741 – 1821). They probably never met but Thrale lived in the later years of her life at Gay Street, Bath and was a noted member of the Blue Stocking Society. From wealthy society - after the death of her first husband, she exercised a complete lack of concern for convention by marrying Gabriel Piozzi, her children's music teacher. Now often acclaimed as an early feminist Hester Thrale is noted for her courage to live an independent lifestyle - with her fashionable salon she entertained artists, poets and thinkers - many mentioned in her own diaries and memories.

Althea also mentions and is very interested in the five More sisters. These independent ladies were Christian educationalists and the most prominent, Hannah More (1745 – 1833) was a member of the Blue Stocking Society. The sisters expanded the work of their father's school in Bristol by opening further schools. By middle age they were living in Great Pulteney Street, Bath and at Wrington in Somerset. All the sisters took a stance against Thomas Paine's republican views manifested through his 'The Rights of Man' but strongly supported William Wilberforce's anti-slavery campaign.

Hannah More had written plays, while moving in the circles of Joshua Reynolds and Samuel Johnson when she was younger but gradually reverted to religious concerns and disassociated herself from 'feminist causes' – being convinced that a woman's independence would not necessarily lead to her happiness.

So, as we compare the interests of all these unusual ladies with those of Althea, they have in common an evangelical interest in education, but with an important caveat - although all advocated rudimentary lessons in reading and writing, most early educationalists did not consider children should be educated beyond the level that might upset the balance of society by increasing expectations.

Perhaps, such opinions lay behind Althea's comments as she reported the various agricultural and industrial riots? How could she have any understanding or sympathy with such Radical politics?

This leads us to perhaps consider what were the topics of conversation during the visit from her three lady cousins from Shabden? Perhaps Catherine Maria Fanshawe had cause to remark…'*Her chief defect is from want of communication with others, which throws her back entirely upon herself & her few concerns & renders her open to such prejudices & too little able to vary her source of ideas with what is passing around her'*… although we know Althea was unwell at that time, but was her patience tested by a slightly younger cousin adopting 'too enlightened' opinions gleaned from 'Blue Stocking' meetings in London?

As always – there are many opinions and agendas within movements for change – especially those around 'feminine' and 'radical' issues.

Whilst researching that last topic another fact emerged which proves that despite an apparent *'want of communication with others'* Althea was talking frequently with a member of the Blue Stocking Society - her close friend 'Mrs' Bowdler'.

So, was Althea influenced by Mrs Bowdler's ideas? No doubt her friend encouraged Althea to continue to write as she herself was engaged in a literary project – editing the plays of Shakespeare. She published versions suitable for children but unfortunately at the time of publication and even now, many literary purists deride her work. The printed copies were popular with the public as soon as they appeared in 1807 as her form of editing did not change the text or plot but merely removed or replaced words considered vulgar or unsuitable for children. This was much in the same way that many fathers were already self-editing when they read aloud to their families.

Originally the lady published under the name of her brother Thomas Bowdler, but his work was mainly on the last plays published. Presumably, he accepted the critical derision on his sister's behalf, but an interesting outcome has ensued, for when 'expurgation' of this type has since been applied in literature, the officially term is 'to Bowdlerise'. Is it not ironic that a word formed out of derision remains and is the continuing legacy for Mrs Bowdler's intensive work and courage to publish?

Nevertheless, Mrs Bowdler has been justified by the many children's versions of classical literature since produced and duly appreciated by generations of children – even though her brother's name is still today, usually credited with her work in addition to his own works regarding European travel.

Connecting these threads of Althea's interests reveal her particular interest in education was most specifically, the education of manners. Her essays in 'Thoughts on Affectation' are the product of a mature mind and perhaps indicates how her illness may have given her opportunities to intensely observe activities when she was unable to 'actively' take part. As she astutely 'interprets' each vice and virtue to correctly weighs the motives and inclinations of her 'characters', she displays a special skill honed and sharpened by time – valuable to any team manager alive today, as she would instinctively know how to place each 'character' in position.

Althea demonstrates a feminine intuition and watchful eye, and by anticipating each new action from the last, whilst she reveals she was 'nobody's fool', by exercising such skills, enemies could easily be made. This ancient, revered talent was once acquired naturally by grandmothers and great-aunts but sadly such talents are too rarely displayed today or respected - yet hopefully all will appreciate Althea's ability to create images with subtle humour.

Extracts from 'Thoughts on Affectation' have been placed between her diary entries in this publication but it is difficult to condense the essence of her work for her 'Thoughts' need time to be browsed and were never intended to be read in one sitting. If you take that time, do not be surprised to find characters familiar to those you know today!

Althea's comments on Public Life

Early in the 19th century, the topics of religion and politics were openly discussed at most levels of society. Money was rapidly moving away from the landowners and into the pockets of the new industrialists and clearly the old order was disappearing. Revolutions in France and America had sent alerts to all, and traditional orthodox religious beliefs were facing challenges from evangelical movements. At Westminster 'Honest Billy'[1] was bent on putting 'honesty' back into politics, and the elite and the clergy's old placement jobs were on the wane.

Among thinking people there was much to discuss, and Althea, like many of her friends was always waiting news from her family absent on army and naval activities. Fortunately, her loyalties were never divided, for although the families of her brother and sister were fighting in different armies, they were fighting the common enemy, Napoleon.

Paradoxically, Althea was so used to her brother's unusual situation that her diary entries give news from Russia in the same easy style as those for British military adventures. Unfazed by distance and unperturbed by foreign parts – possibly she reflected Britain's global reach and the nation's confidence as a naval superpower?

Althea provides details of an expansive range of public events all now referenced as footnotes on the diary pages – follow them as you are inclined – but perhaps her commentary on the matrimonial scandals of the Georgian royal family will be too tempting to ignore. Of course, reminiscent of today, but the amount of information available to the public via the newspapers is quite surprising.

In this bicentennial year of Althea Fanshawe's death hopefully some will be curious to read her diary – and with her 'unnecessary' gaps now filled her entries have context – but still you must make your own assessment of the diary's value.

---

[1] Prime Minister William Pitt, the younger.

Althea's 'lists of facts' ultimately provide us with her story in an unusual way - but uniquely all are coloured by her 'view' from a narrow window with wide horizons.

Deirdre Marculescu
December 2024.

Custodians of the Diary

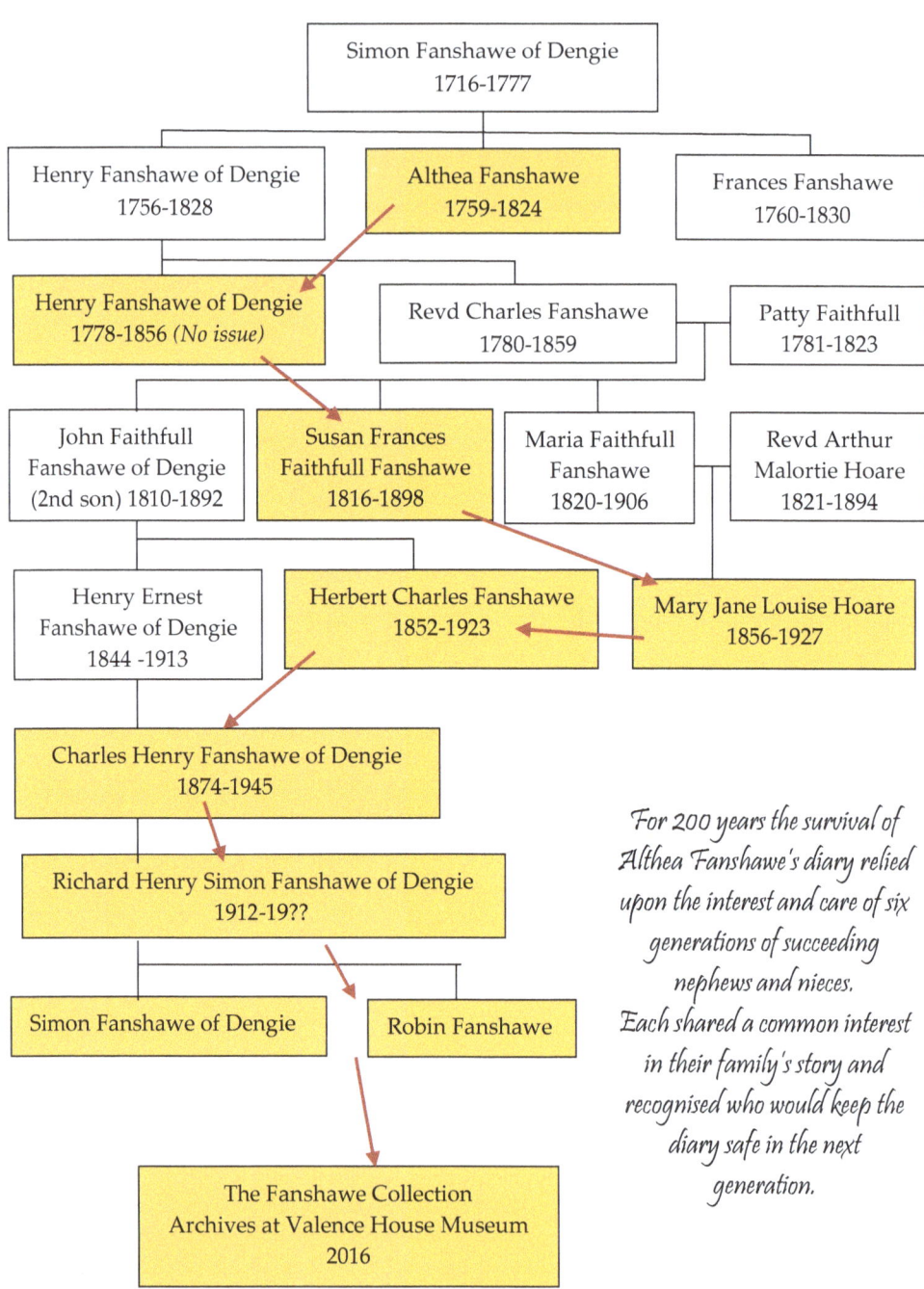

For 200 years the survival of Althea Fanshawe's diary relied upon the interest and care of six generations of succeeding nephews and nieces. Each shared a common interest in their family's story and recognised who would keep the diary safe in the next generation.

Transcriber's notes

Althea Fanshawe laid out her diary in an efficient and orderly way which allows any reader to follow her notes. Once the original was scanned, and enlarged on the computer screen, her handwriting has become mostly readable after making allowances for her idiosyncrasies of style.

The original diary is laid out in exactly the format as seen in this edition, including the small lines in column boxes denoting a birth, marriage or a death. Althea also included an index of those events at the end of her diary, giving her quick reference to the year. For this publication that index was not considered appropriate and it was hoped that a fuller index of all events and names could be included. However once that project was commenced it was discovered that any such index would be so extensive that it would grow beyond any usefulness. Any researcher into births, marriages and deaths within the period of the diary should easily be able to locate the information by the use of Althea's methodical tables. With regard to public events - the date of that event becomes the point of reference to the diary.

Althea's inclusion of many unfamiliar names relating to people, places and events presented the main challenge. Fortunately, knowledge of the Fanshawe family pedigree, has initially been an advantage but for the many unfamiliar names, extensive research became necessary.

Resulting from this study, many new facts have come to light concerning Althea's wider family. Also interesting, have been her acquaintances and friends and the many personalities of the period which she mentions. With this new information, Althea's life may now be viewed within a far wider context.

It is my hope that the references included will spark interest from other researchers with their own areas of interest and at Valence House Museum there will always be interest to know where and how Althea Fanshawe's observations contribute.

Few abbreviations are used in this transcription but for ease of reading and to avoid constant repetition, the following apply:-

AF	Althea Fanshawe – Diarist
HCF	Herbert Charles Fanshawe – author of 'The History of the Fanshawe Family'
HFF	Publication - The History of the Fanshawe Family.
[--]	Insertions to the original made by transcriber.
My Brother	Henry - AF's only brother (with capital B), never referred to by name (he and his sister Francis both had sons named Henry - usually referred to with their surname).
My Sister	Francis - AF's only sister (with capital S), never referred to by name (her sister's daughter Francis is usually called Fanny).
<u>Words</u>	Underlined as appears in the original.
~~Words~~	Stuck out words as appears in the original.

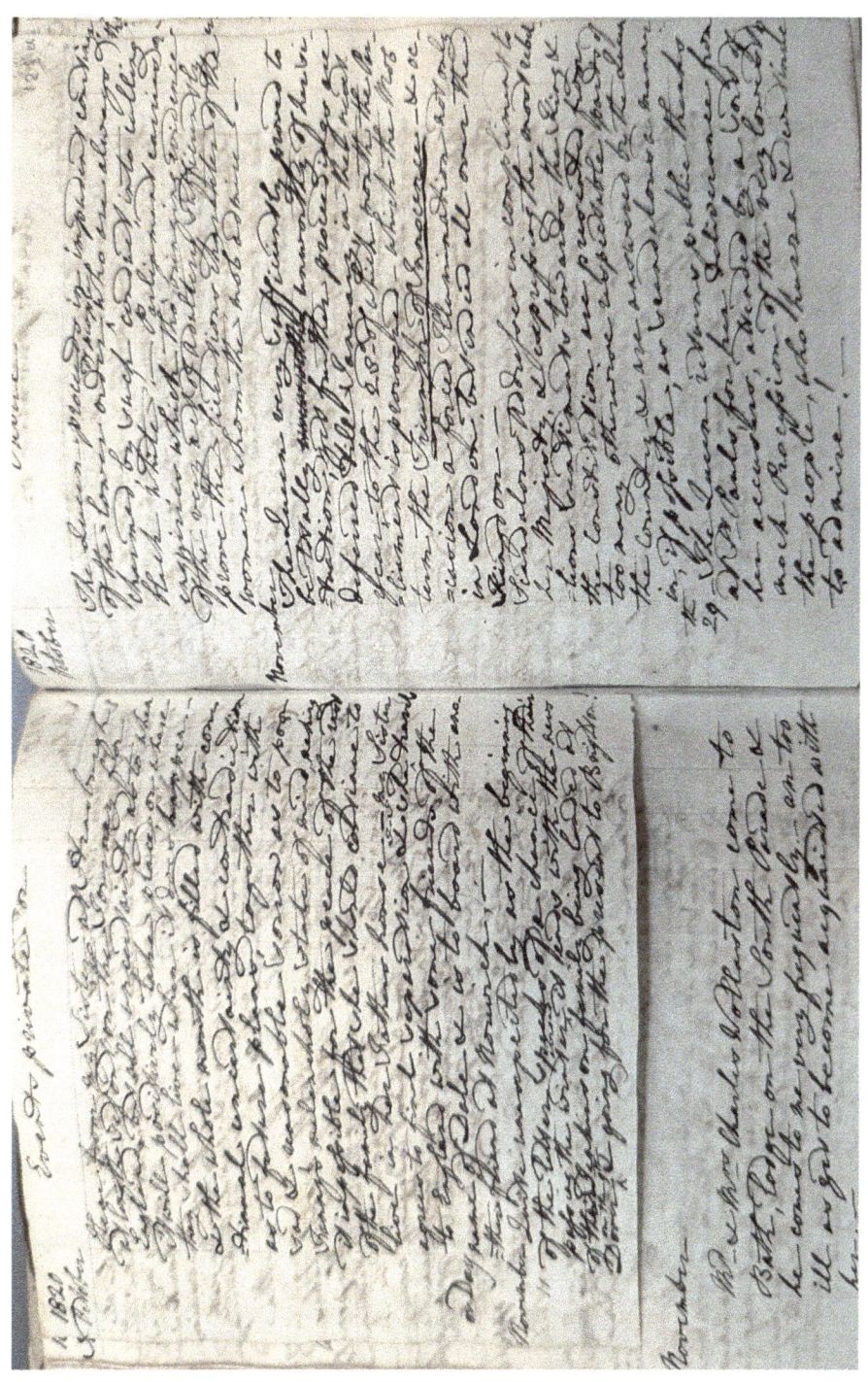

Photograph copy of a page from Althea's diary entries

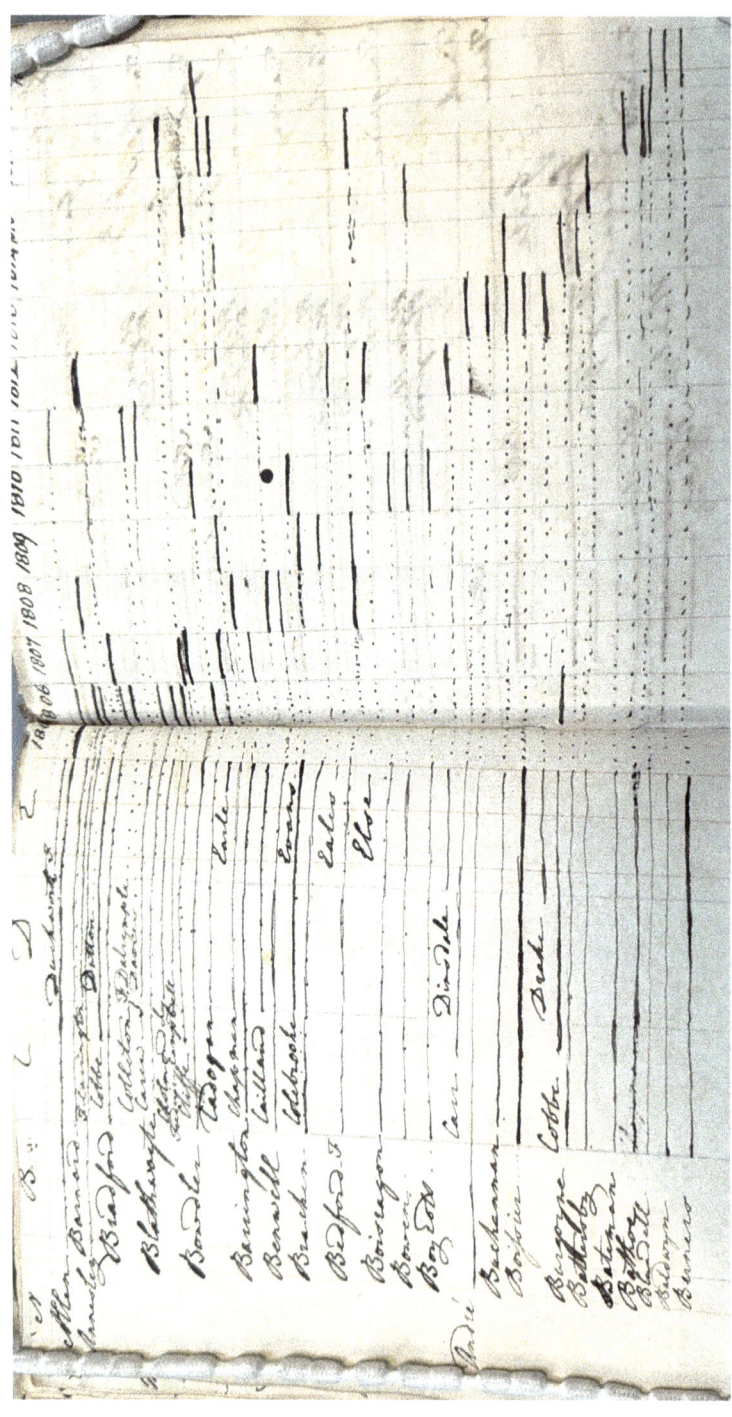

Photograph copy of a page from Althea's diary index

'I have not begun this with any degree of sanity till a year & four months after our mother's death.

I am determined on it as I can, to make out the deficiency of this time by recollection - & for the future keep up her custom of noting all family occurrences & such amongst my acquaintance & public facts, as may happen to take me. Death & marriages of acquaintance is certainly particularly convenient to write down as it is sometime very useful to <u>happen</u> to know when any <u>happened,</u> which are a sort I almost constantly forget.'

1806 – May 13

A record of events for the years

1805 - 1824

1805
Family events & circumstances relative to myself alone.

January 2	My sister[1] & Fanny Jenkinson arrived about noon.
8	This was the day of my beloved Mother's[2] internment.
9	My Sister, Fanny & Charles[3] left me.
19	Took my oath as Executrix to my Mother's Will.
30	Charles returned.
February 24	Charles left me.
March 25	Settled with Mr Cruttwell[4] about printing my new book.
	Mrs Hosier[5] left the bulk of her property to the Jenkinsons which it is imagined by my Sister will amount to between 7 or 8000£. stock and to my Brother & myself £300 stock each with some other trifling legacies to other people.
August 9	Charles returned.
Sept 29	[6]Commenced as Tenant to Mr Pennicott from Michaelmas day.
October 26	Doctor Parry[7] began Oil of Amber once more.

---

[1] Frances (Fanshawe) Jenkinson (1760-1830) & her daughter, Frances (Fanny).
[2] AF's mother Althea (Snelling) Fanshawe, buried with her husband in Bath Abbey, was his 1st cousin, being the daughter of William Snelling of Bromley St Leonards, a member of the Levant Co.
[3] Charles Robert Fanshawe (1780-1859) - 2nd son of AF's brother General Henry Fanshawe (Russian Service).
[4] Richard Cruttwell, printer of many & various books and the newspaper 'The Bath Chronicle'.
[5] 9th March (probate) in respect of Elizabeth Hosier, half sister of AF's father and child of Elizabeth, widow of Thomas Edward Fanshawe (1691-1726) and her 2nd husband Edward Hosier.
[6] This entry was inserted separately on the facing page of the diary.
[7] Caleb Hillier Parry, M.D. whose consulting rooms were at 27 The Circus, Bath.

November 16	Day of Charles's marriage[1].
December	Published my 'Thoughts on Affectations' in the course of this year[2] but exactly when I cannot remember (I think November).
	Henry Fanshawe is made a Lieutenant & went out to the West Indies to join the Oquijo[3] but happily did not arrive till after the misfortune of the loss of the vessel.

Fits 29 - Attacks 152

Dr Caleb Hillier Parry
(1755-1822)

---

[1] Date of marriage at Warfield, Berkshire officially recorded as 4th November 1805.
[2] No date other than 1805 is included on this published book.
[3] Previously a Spanish corvette, the Royal Navy's sloop O[r]quijo foundered off Port Antonio, Jamaica on 7th November 1805, when most of the crew were lost.

1805
Family marriages, deaths or births.

		Marriages	Deaths	Births
January 1	My dear & most excellent Mother[1]		—	
February	Sir Thomas Rivers[2]		—	
March	Miss Hosier[3]		—	
	Miss Hyde & Mr Hamilton[4]	—		
April	Miss M Rivers to Capt. Stephenson[5]	—		
July	Mrs Henry Wollaston[6]		—	
August	Miss Rivers to Mr Freeling[7]	—		
October	Sir James Rivers[8]		—	
November 16	Charles Robert Fanshawe to Miss Faithfull[9]	—		

---

[1] 1st January - Mrs Althea Fanshawe died on the 26th anniversary of her husband's death.
[2] 3rd February - Sir Thomas Rivers Gay, 7th Baronet (1770-1805) of Walcot, Bath.
[3] Miss Hosier died at Richmond Buildings in Soho - she left an extensive will with AF named as executrix and included are many details of bequests, investments & property.
[4] 2nd April - Maria Catherine Hyde of Droxford, Southampton married Augustus B.P.P Hamilton at St Georges' Westminster.
[5] Maria Rivers daughter of Sir Peter Rivers Gay 6th Bt. married Benjamin Stephenson (later Major General Sir) who died 1839.
[6] 25th July - Mary Ann (Blanke-Nilagen) Wollaston - 1st wife of H S Wollaston.
[7] 20th August - Emilia Henrietta Rivers to Francis Freeling (1764-1836) - at Winchester.
[8] 27th September - brother of ([5] above) - 8th Baronet (1772-1805).
[9] Patty Faithfull, daughter of Revd Robert Faithfull (1781-1823), Vicar of Warfield, Berkshire.

1805
Marriages, Deaths or Births among Acquaintances or neighbours.

	Marriages	Deaths	Births
Miss Parry to Mr Garnier[1]	—		
Miss C Mason		—	

The Dean's Garden - Winchester

---

[1] 6th May - Mary Parry, daughter of AF's doctor married Revd Thomas Garnier (1776-1873). He was also a botantist and created 'The Dean's Garden' while he held that post at Winchester Cathedral.

1805
Events Private.

[None recorded]

1805
Events public.

So many wonderful events so well recorded in so many ways this year took place, that not having begun the custom so soon as I wished I had, I shall not write down any of the circumstances which I think never can escape my memory.

*The Battle of Trafalgar - 21st October 1805
by Clarkson Frederick Stanfield*

1806
Family Events & Circumstances relative to myself alone.

February 7	Charles & Mrs Charles Fanshawe came.
March 13	Doctor Parry gives up Oil of Amber.
April 21	Charles & Mrs Charles Fanshawe left me.
May	Henry Fanshawe[1] returned to England.
13	News from my Brother that he has the Great Cross of St Vladimir given him - that his son William is gone with Ministerial dispatches to Vienna & that Frederic has an appointment with the Russian Ambassador at Constantinople of 500 hundred roubles pr.ann.
June	Henry Fanshawe garrisons in the Shaldrake, removes to the Courageux in Sir J B Warrens'[2] Squadron.
	Edward Jenkinson[3] a Lieutenancy in the Colour team.
July	Charles & his wife settle at Dengie Hall.
August	News from Henry off the Madeiras - well & in good spirits.
	Charles & his wife return from Dengie to Warfield for her to lay in there.
September	My sister & Fanny Jenkinson in great danger from the sore throat which destroyed Elinor & with which more of the family were affected.
October	Mrs Charles brought to bed of a son[4].
	Henry Fanshawe returns to England with Sir J B Warren.
November	Henry Jenkinson[1] sails in the Decade frigate for

---

[1] Eldest son of AF's brother - Rear Admiral Henry Fanshawe (1778-1856).
[2] Admiral Sir John Borlase Warren, 1st Baronet GCB GCH PC (1753-1822).
[3] AF's nephew and a son of John & Frances Jenkinson (died 1809).
[4] 9th October - Charles Simon Faithfull Fanshawe (1806-1873).

	America.
December	The Jenkinson family after long and repeated returns of the dreadful illness they reaffected from in September, leave Kensington and London for the sea shore in hopes of benefit from change of air.
	News of Mrs Fanshawe's death at Caffa[2] in September.
	Charles S F Fanshawe vaccinated.[3]

Fits 29 - Attacks 130

Imperial Order of Saint Vladimir

---

[1] Henry Jenkinson (1790-1865) a son of Frances & John Jenkinson - retired 1814 as Captain.
[2] Susanna Frances (1754-1806) daughter & co-heir of Charles Le Grys and wife of AF's brother Henry, died at Caffa (Kaffa), Crimea.
[3] Vaccination against smallpox was pioneered by Edward Jenner, a close friend and colleague of Dr Caleb Parry.

1806
Family Marriages, Deaths or Births.

		Marriages	Deaths	Births
February	Miss Louisa Wollaston[1] to Revd J L Jackson	—		
	Mr John Charles Fanshawe[2] to Miss Carrington	—		
June	Bishop of Limerick (Barnard) [3]		—	
September	Elizabeth Jenkinson - putrid sore throat		—	
	Miss Penelope Fanshawe[4] to Major Duckworth	—		
October	Mrs Charles Fanshawe brought to bed of a son, Charles Simon Faithfull			—
December	Mrs Fanshawe, my Brother's wife, at Kaffa[5] September 6th tho' the news has but just reached us in a letter from my Brother to Mr Sharp[6]		—	

---

[1] 4th February - Lousia Decima Hyde Wollaston, youngest surviving daughter of (approx.) 18 children of Revd Francis Wolleston & Althea Hyde, married Rev'd James Leonard Jackson.
[2] John C Fanshawe (1780-1830) eldest son of Charles Fanshawe (1742-1784) Recorder of Exeter married Frances Delia Carrington (d.1854).
[3] Thomas Barnard (c.1726/28-1806) a member of the Literary Club, and friend of Samuel Johnson, Oliver Goldsmith, Sir Joshua Reynolds & Edmund Burke.
[4] Penelope Fanshawe (1789-1855) a daughter of Capt. Robert Fanshawe RN, Commissioner of Plymouth Dockyard, married Major George H Duckworth.
[5] Kaffa (Theodosia) Crimea [as noted in original diary by H C Fanshawe].
[6] British Consul in St Petersburgh.

1806

Marriages, Deaths or Births amongst Acquaintances & neighbours.

		Marriages	Deaths	Births
	Lady Bradford[1]		—	
	Mrs Anne Northey[2]		—	
	Suddenly, Mrs Hanbury Williams[3]		—	
	Mr Bishop - (Master) of White Knights[4]		—	
May	Suddenly Mr Bathurst Pye[5]		—	
	Lady Betsy Cobbe[6]		—	
	Miss Louisa Phillott to Mr Fuge[7]	—		
	Almost suddenly Mr Blathwayt[8]		—	
June	Lt. Col. Villez, by jumping out of a coach		—	
August	Mr Palmer of Holme Park, Surrey[9]		—	

---

[1] Elizabeth, Lady Bridgeman, afterwards Lady Bradford (1735-1806).
[2] Probably Mary Anne Northey of Bath died April 1806 at the family seat at Box, Wiltshire.
[3] Elizabeth (Jones) wife of John Hanbury Williams.
[4] Whiteknights Park near Reading - then owned by the Marquis of Blandford.
[5] 4th May - William Bathurst Pye of Salthrop, Wiltshire (1764-1806).
[6] 6th May - Lady Elizabeth Cobbe (1736-1806) wife of Col.Thomas Cobbe MP & daughter of 1st Earl of Tyrone.
[7] 1st May - Mary Louisa E Phillott & Robert Fuge, a merchant of Plymouth married at Bath.
[8] Rev'd (George) William Blathwayt of Dyrham Park, Gloucestershire (1751-1806).
[9] 29th July - Richard Palmer who rebuilt Holme Park where the gardens were later landscaped by Humphrey Repton.

	Mr Colleton formerly Garth of Haines Hill to Miss Carew[1]		
September	Mr Thomas Bowdler formerly Dr Bowdler to Mrs Trevennan[2]	—	
October	Miss Cholmondeley[3] overturned in an open carriage with the Princess of Wales.	—	
	Mrs Freeman of Henley Park[4]	—	
	Mr Thomas Rooper[5] to [-]	—	

> This day is published, in 10 vols. royal 18mo, price 3l. 3s. boards, THE FAMILY SHAKSPEARE: in which nothing is added to the original Text: but those words and expressions are omitted which cannot with propriety be read aloud in a Family. By THOMAS BOWDLER, Esq., F. R. S. and S. A. "My great objects in this undertaking are to remove from the writings of Shakspeare, some defects which diminish their value; and, at the same time, to present to the public an edition of his Plays, which the parent, the guardian, and the instructor of youth, may place without fear in the hands of the pupil; and from which the pupil may derive instruction as well as pleasure; may improve his moral principles, while he refines his taste; and without incurring the danger of being hurt with any indelicacy of expression, may learn in the fate of Macbeth, that even a kingdom is dearly purchased, if virtue be the price of acquisition."—Preface. Printed for Longman, Hurst, Rees, Orme, and Brown, London.

[1] 17th July - Charles Garth Colleton of Haynes Hill, Berkshire married Charlotte Pole-Carew, daughter of Rt. Hon. Reginald Pole-Carew.

[2] 13th September - Thomas Bowdler (1754-1824) & Mrs Elizabeth Trevannan. This marriage proved to be unhappy and the couple soon separated. Bowdler and his sister Henrietta Bowdler (1750-1830) published 'sanitised' versions of Shakespeare and other writers - resulting in this type of correction to artistic work since being termed as 'to Bowdlerise'. Also a noted player of chess, Thomas Bowdler gave his name to the 'Bowdler Attack'.

[3] 2nd October - While Harriet Mary Cholmondeley was accompanying Princess Charlotte to Norbury Park, Leatherhead, the driver overturned the carriage at a tight bend which brought about her death.

[4] 6th October - Sarah (née Winsford) widow of Sambrooke Freeman MP - owner of Hawley Court, Henley and the Living of Fawley..

[5] Revd Thomas Rooper, Rector of Abbots Ripton - married Persis Standly.

1806
Events Private.

[None recorded]

Generosity

This is not to be confined to bestowing alms or making presents; for in that case it would belong to those alone who have from riches the power of conferring pecuniary gifts; whilst those who are poor, yet with equally open hearts, would be excluded from the exercise of a virtue which takes a far wider scope, and is quite as discoverable in the low as in the high stations... AF

1806
Events Public.

I have begun only in May.	Lord Melvilles' Trial[1]
June	Lord Melville acquitted
	Princess of Wales accused[2].
August	Victory in Calabria under General Stewart[3]
September	Conquest (in May) of [4]Buenos A[i]yres by Sir Homes Popham & death of Lord Thurlow.
	Death of Mr Fox[5]
October	Four French frigates taken by Sir Samuel Hood[6] who lost his arm in the action - and one by Sir Thomas Louis[7]
October	End to the Negotiation for Peace with France.

---

[1] Henry Dundas, 1st Viscount Melville, PC, FRSE (1742-1811) was the confidente of Prime Minister William Pitt. As the younger and most important politician in Scotland at this time, he was an abolitionist and powerful leader of the Scottish Enlightenment. Impeachment proceedings began against him in 1806 relating to misappropriation of funds while in office as Treasurer of the Navy and although acquitted, his political career came to an end.

[2] By 1806 the Prince Regent and his wife had lived apart for 10 years and rumours were circulating that the Princess had taken lovers.

[3] 4th July - The Battle of Maida, under General John Stuart.

[4] British invasion of the River Plate in the Anglo Spanish War 1796-1808.

[5] 13th September - Charles James Fox (1749-1806), prominent Whig politician.

[6] 25th September - battle fought off the French Biscay port of Rochefort - a French squadron of five frigates and two corvettes bound with supplies for the French West Indies was intercepted by a British squadron of six ships under the command of Commodore Sir Samuel Hood.

[7] 6th February - Admiral Sir Thomas Louis, 1st Bt. (1758-1807) fought in the Battle of San Domingo.

October	Defeat of the Russian Army by the French
	Death of the Duke of Brunswick[1] owing to a wound when the Russians were defeated.

Caroline of Brunswick,, Princess of Wales
(Sir Thomas Lawrence 1798)
Victoria & Albert Museum

---

[1] Charles, Duke of Brunswick (1735-1806) died from a musket ball wound at the Battle of Jena-Auersted. He and his wife Princess Augusta, a sister of King George III, were the parents of the estranged wife of the Prince of Wales, later King George IV.

1807
Family events & circumstances relative to myself alone.

	Jenkinson Family at Brighthelmestone[1]
January 30	Charles, his wife & child came to me.
February	Mr F Wollaston[2] chosen Master of Sydney College Cambridge
April 7	Charles, his wife & child leave me to go to Warfield in their way to Dengie
19	Charles finding his house not likely to be ready for him, takes a lodging at Maldon for 3 months beginning from 1st of June.
	Dr Parry determined to leave off medicines for sometime.
May	£144.3. p^d at consolidated annuities transferred to me by the New Jersey Society being my dividend on 18 shares at £8 p^r share.
	Col^l Jenkinson[3] restored to his Inspectorship.
June July August	My brother leaves Petersburgh & returned to the Crimea with the command of all the Forces on the East Side of the Dnieper - his third son William who had been severely wounded in the face was recovering when he wrote his letter which was to Charles.
	[Note - The diary has a slip of paper covering the above section for June to August on which is written the following:]
June	Obliged to return to medicine.

---

[1] This original name of the coastal town of Brighton was officially retained until 1810. Introduction of the shortened name only began in the middle of 17th century.
[2] 2nd cousin - Francis John Hyde Wollaston FRS (1762-1823), Philosopher, Jacksonian Professor and Master of Sydney Sussex College.
[3] Lt. General John Jenkinson (1757-1830) husband of AF's sister Frances - appointed Inspecting Officer of Volunteers in 1811.

July	Jenkinson family remove to Epsom where they have taken a house till November.
August	Much more ill than common, owing to having caught cold whilst I was taking a mascunial medicine and a stop put to everything by this means. Somewhat better & medicines again attempted.
December	A stop to medicines - immediately considerably worse. Obliged to return to medicine

Francis John Hyde Wollaston

1807
Family Marriages, Deaths & Births.

		Marriages	Deaths	Births
March	Mr Edward Jenkinson[1], brother to Col^{l.} Jenkinson		—	
April	Mrs Jackson, of a boy			—
	Mrs Mary Cliffe		—	
	Mrs Fanshawe[2] of Shabden		—	
July	Mr Edward Faithfull, brother to Mrs C Fanshawe		—	
	Mrs Duckworth, of a daughter			—
August	Mr Rivers of Winchester[3]		—	
October 15	Mrs C Fanshawe of a <u>boy</u> [4]			—
30	Henry Fanshawe		—	
November	Miss Althea Heberden[5] to Rev'^d Mr Karslake	—		

Fits 26 - Attacks 144

---

[1] 27th March (burial) - Rev'd Edward Jenkinson at Alveston, Warwickshire.
[2] Penelope, wife of John Fanshawe of Shadden (1738-1807) - daughter of John Dredge & mother of the poet, Catherine Maria Fanshawe.
[3] Possibly a younger brother of Sir Peter Rivers (later Rivers Gay).
[4] Charles & Patty Fanshawe's child Henry died 15 days later.
[5] 18th November - Althea Heberden, granddaughter of Francis Wollaston married William Karslake, Rector of Dolton Devon & Canon of St. Peter's Cathedral, Exeter.

1807

Marriages, deaths or births amongst acquaintances or neighbours.

		Marriages	Deaths	Births
January	Mrs Duttons[1] - Miss K Gubbins - this was of delirious fever three days only after her appearing in her usual showy dashing stile!		—	
	~~Mrs Whalley of the Crescent~~ (see October)		—	
	Mrs Long[2] of Gay Street		—	
	Lady Hesketh[3]		—	
March	Doctor Taylor of Reading to Miss J Manley[4]	—		
	Col¹ Parker to Miss W Roterholme	—		
	Miss Jane Allen[5] of Greenwich - 90 years old		—	
April	Dr Malone of the Charter House		—	
	Lord Cadogan[6]		—	

---

[1] An extract of a letter dated 1803 by Mrs Philip Lybbe Powys gives more information of the lady: 'In March, Mr (Ralph) Dutton, brother to Lord Sherbourne married at Bath the celebrated beauty, Miss Honoria Gubbins'. Miss Gubbins seems to have come from a dubious background and was depicted in a 1793 satirical print 'The Bath Beauties' now held by the British Museum.
[2] 24th March - Mrs Anne Long buried at Walcot.
[3] Harriet Ashley Cowper (1733-1807), daughter of Ashley Cowper (1701-1788) was the wife of Sir Thomas Hesketh. She was a cousin and close friend of the poet and writer William Cowper.
[4] 10th March - Dr John Taylor & Maria Manley married at Reading.
[5] 26th March - buried at St Alfege's Greenwich.
[6] Charles Sloane Cadogan, 1st Earl Cadogan (1728-1807) a British Whig politician.

	Mr King[1] - the author of many religious works	—	
May	Mr Mason[2] of Queens Parade	—	
July	Lady Frederick Campbell[3] (formerly) Lady (Ferrers) burnt to death [with] part of the house she was in near Tunbridge, also the fire beginning in her room where she was sitting up after the rest of the family were in bed.	—	
August	Mrs Barrington[4], wife of the Bishop of Durham	—	
September	Mrs Maltby of The Crescent[5]	—	
	Doctor Fraser[6]	—	
October	Mrs Whalley[7] of The Crescent	—	

---

[1] Edward King (1735-1807) barrister and writer known for his works relating to castles and antiquities - he also published some controversial religious books.
[2] 30th May - John Mason, Esq - buried at St Swithin's Church Walcot.
[3] Mary Shirley, Countess Ferrers (c.1730-1807), formerly Mary Meredith, later wife of Sir Frederick Campbell, brother of the Duke of Argyll - died at Coombe Bank, Kent.
[4] Jane, only daughter of Sir John Guise, Bart, who died 1807, was the wife of Shute Barrington (1734-1826), successively Bishop of Llandaff, Salisbury, and Durham.
[5] 19th September - Elizabeth Maltby of Royal Crescent died aged 81.
[6] Dr William Mackinen Fraser moved to London in 1799 after practising at Southampton and Bath. Shortly before his death he was appointed physician extraordinary to the Prince of Wales.
[7] Miss Heathcote, a lady with property in Wiltshire and 2nd wife of English cleric, poet and traveller Thomas Sedgwick Whalley (1746-1828).

	Edward Golding jnr.[1] to Miss Frances Bowles	—		
December	Mrs Pigott[2] of Northumberland Buildings	—		
	Mrs Tobin[3], St James Parade			

The Field of Mars - St Petersburg 1807
by Benjamin Patersen (died 1815)

---

[1] 7th November - Edward Golding JP, DL (died 1844) of Sunning, Berks the son of the Rt Hon. Edward Golding, M.P., Lord of the Treasury during Lord Sidmouth's administration - married Frances Bowles.
[2] 3rd December - Mrs Elizabeth Piggott (1742-1807).
[3] 22nd December - Mrs Mary Tobin buried in Bath Abbey.

1807
Events private.

January	Henry Fanshawe sails in the Courageux under Rear Admiral Lewis
February	Doctor Fraser[1] leaves London owing to illness.
April	Henry Jenkinson sails for the West Indies - his destination changed to the Madeiras. William Fanshawe wounded in the face by a musket thro' the which carries away all his teeth on the right side & he is Brigade Adjutant in the Russian Army now opposing the French.
May	My Brother leaves Petersburgh & returns towards Crimea with the command of all the forces to the East of the Dnieper.
June	Henry Jenkinson returns to England.
July	H J sails again in the Decade Corps Stewards
	Edward Jenkinson goes with the expedition on board the London - Capt. Cumberland[2].
September	Henry Jenkinson returns to England.
October	Henry Jenkinson sails again for Cork same vessel.
November	Edward Jenkinson returns to England.
December	Mr Charles Phillots[3] appointed to a living worth £300 p.ann near Bath.

---

[1] Presumably Dr. William Fraser practicing at Bath from 1787-98 who also served on Bath City Council.
[2] Capt. Willam Cumberland was in command of the Leyden on 7th August off Helsingørat at the Battle of Copenhagen.
[3] Charles Phillott (1774-1851) appointed Vicar of Badsey & Wickhamford during March 1808, was absent for most of the time, as he also held the Livings of Frome and Teignmouth.

1807
Events public.

January	Buenos Ayres retaken by the Spaniards.
February	Victory of the Russians over the French - this is a most bloody action after which both armies retired & each claim the Victory?
	Abolition of Slave Trade[1].
March	Trial of Sir Home Popham[2] for having acted contrary to orders when he took Buenos Ayres - acquitted of positive guilt, but severely reprimanded!
	Complete change of Ministry - Duke of Portland[3] now at the head.
April	Capture of Montevideo[4] - by Sir S Achmutz & Admiral Hirling.
	Dissolution of Parliament.
June	Meeting of the new Parliament.
July	Decided Victory of the French over the Russians[5] which produced an immediate Armistice asked for by the defeated party.
	Duchess of Brunswick[6] comes to reside in England.
	Peace[1] concluded between Russia, Prussia & France.

---

[1] 25th March - after a lengthy campaign led by William Wilberforce, the Abolition of the Slave Trade Act was signed into law by King George III.

[2] 6th March - Capt. Sir Home Popham RN tried for neglect of duty for leaving the Cape of Good Hope unprotected whilst Commander of a squadron to take the Cape and then cruize off the station. His court martial was held on board HMS Gladiator.

[3] Prime Minister William Cavendish-Bentinck, 3rd Duke of Portland (1738-1809) beginning his 3rd separate term of government.

[4] 3rd February - the Battle of Montevideo.

[5] 20th June - an armistice was agreed after the Grande Armée defeated the Russians at Friedland - the peace treaty was signed by Czar Alexander I & Napoleon at Tilsit on 7 July.

[6] Marie of Baden (1782-1808), Duchess of Brunswick-Wolfenbüttel & Brunswick-Oels; wife of Frederick William, Duke of Brunswick-Wolfenbüttel, close friend of King George IV.

August	Death of the Duchess of Gloucester.[2]
September	Defeat of English Troops in South America[3] - forced to give up Monte Video & to remove from the Rio de la Plata with a loss of upwards of 1100 men - Sir S Auchmutz & Gen. Crawford returned to England.
	Surrender of Copenhagen[4] & of the whole Danish Fleet to the British forces under Admiral Gambier & Lord Cathcart.
October	Return to England
November	Strange arrival of Louis 18th[5] in England.
December	Russia declares enmity - war determined upon.
	Departure of the Portuguese Royal Family[6] for South America under English protection.

---

[1] 7th July - see Treaty of Tilsit at [5] above.

[2] 22nd August - Maria, Duchess of Gloucester and Edinburgh (1736-1807) widow of Prince William Henry, Duke of Gloucester and Edinburgh, a younger brother of King George III.

[3] Battles fought as part of the British invasion of the River Plate against the Spanish during the Napoleonic Wars. The British having captured Buenos Aires in 1806 followed with success at the Battle of Montevideo but were forced eventually to surrender (September 1807).

[4] 16th August - 7th September - The Battle of Copenhagen when the British captured and destroyed the Danish fleet at Copenhagan during the Napoleonic Wars.

[5] Louis XVIII who had been under the protection of the Tzar in Russia, found his safety could no longer be assured and left for Stockholm in July 1807. Then he travelled on and arrived at Great Yarmouth, England during November that year. After staying first at Gosfield Hall in Essex, he later moved to Hartwell House, Bucks - where he remained until the French Restoration in 1814.

[6] 27th November - Queen Maria I of Portugal with John, the Prince Regent and the entire Braganza royal family, left Lisbon with a court of almost 10,000 bound for the Portuguese colony of Brazil. Their departure was just four days before Napoleon's forces invaded Portugal.

1808
Family events & circumstance relative to myself.

January	Jenkinson Family came to London where the Colonel has taken a house for two months in York Place, Baker Street.
19	Charles, his wife & child come to me - [his xxxxx xxx handed down to pxxxxxxy].
March	They leave me & proceed to Warfield in their way to Dengie.
26	Stop to medicine for fits, owing to a vicious cold.
April	£2000 Orphan Stock[1] paid off to me with which I bought £3100 sp - in reduced annuities
6	Charles arrives at Dengie to settle; his wife and child to follow.
May	Seized with Rheumatism from which I suffer considerable & consequently prevented from returning to medicine for the Fits, which Dr Parry was then planning.
30	Begin a new medicine for my fits.
June 21	Forced to leave off the new medicine by a return of Rheumatism
22	My Sister writes word that by means of Sir S Sharp[2] she is informed of my brother being dismissed the Russian service on half pay.
July 9	Begin a fresh medicine for my fits.
	Col.l Jenkinson takes Combe Cottage near Croydon in Surrey for his family.

---

[1] Widow & Orphan Stock - in stock markets, a type that reliably provide regular dividends whilst yielding slow but steady rise in market value over the longer term.
[2] British Consul in St Petersburg.

August 14	Agree with Mr Hatchard[1] about printing my 'Sunday of Reflections'.
October 17	Receive the first proof sheet from Mr Hatchard.
November 3	Heard in a round-a-bout way by means of Lady Douglas[2] that my brother was at Petersburgh where herself is just recovered from a very alarming illness.
21	Mr Wolstenholme of Derbyshire offers me £100 if I would sell the perpetuity of the Free School[3]
December 21	Returned the two last proofs.
29	Mr Hatchard promised my copies in a week & fixes the price of the book at 9s-
30	Heard of Edward Jenkinson going to Ramsgate in order to sail with the expedition.
	Heard by means of the Sharps of my brother at Petersburgh in August - having taken a house to live there with an establishment.

*John Hatchard
Publisher & Bookseller*

---

[1] John Hatchard (1769-1849) founder of the publishing house and bookshop in Piccadilly, London that still trades today. As the main publisher of evangelical works, his premises were a meeting place for social reformers.

[2] The wife of the Marquis of Douglas & Clydesdale sent in 1807 to St. Petersburg as British Ambassador extrordinaire.

[3] Dronfield Grammar School, founded in 1568 under the terms of the Will of Henry Fanshawe. Set up by his nephew, the direct ancestor of AF - Thomas Fanshawe, 2nd Remembrancer of the Exchequer to Queen Elizabeth I.

1808
Family Marriages Deaths & Births.

		Marriages	Deaths	Births
January	Andrew Barnard[1] at the Cape of Good Hope, son to the late Bishop of Limerick		—	
	Miss Susan Fanshawe[2] to Captain Bedford of the Navy.	—		
	Mrs Jackson of a girl.			—
June	Mrs Nichols of a girl.[3]			—
September	Mrs George Wollaston[4] of a girl.			—
	Mrs Karslake[5] of a boy.			—
November 27	Ms C Fanshawe of a daughter, Althea[6].			—

Fits 22 - Attacks 175

---

[1] 27th October - death of Andrew Barnard (1762-1807), Secretary to the Colony of Cape of Good Hope.

[2] 13th January - Susan (1774-1855) daughter of Capt Robert Fanshawe RN, Commissioner of Plymouth Dockyard, married Admiral William Bedford (1766-1827).

[3] 8th June (baptism) probably Martha daughter of Francis & Mary Nichols of Walcot.

[4] Mrs Mary Anne Wollaston nee Luard of Witham Lodge Essex.

[5] 18th September (baptism) - William Heberden Karslake.

[6] 8th January 1809 (baptism) - Althea Faithfull Fanshawe at Warfield.

1808
Marriages, Deaths or Births amongst acquaintances or neighbours.

		Marriages	Deaths	Births
February	Mr Scott of Danesfield[1]		—	
	Dr Chapman[2] President of Trinity College, Oxford		—	
March	Dr Hind of Sussex to Mrs Benwell formerly Miss Loveday[3]	—		
April	Mrs Ross[4] of the Circus		—	
May	Miss Emma Parry to Mr Eardley Wilmot[5]	—		
August	Lt. Col. Taylor[6] - son to Dr Taylor of Reading, killed in Portugal		—	
September	Lady Rich[7]		—	
October	Mrs Caillaud[8] of Aston, Oxfordshire		—	
	Mrs Levreson Gower,		—	

---

[1] Robert Scott (1746-1808) MP for parliments 1774 & 1780, lived at Danesfield House, Buckinghamshire.

[2] Revd.Dr Joseph Chapman, President of Trinity College 1776-1808 & Vice-Chancellor of Oxford 1784/88.

[3] 18th March - Penelope Loveday (1759-1846) first married to William Benwell, Rector of Chilton was married secondly in 1808 to John Hind, Vicar of Findon Sussex. Diaries kept by this lady for the years 1787-1838 have been published.

[4] 12th April - Elizabeth Ross buried at St Swithin Churchyard, Bath.

[5] 18th May - Emma Parry, (daughter of AF's doctor & friend) married John Eardley Wilmot (1821 - 1st Bt Eardley-Wilmot) - a politician and colonial administrator who from 1843-1846 was Lt. Governor of Van Diemen's Land *(Tasmania)*.

[6] 21st August - Commanding Officer of the 20th Light Dragoons was killed in the Battle of Vimiera.

[7] Ann Willis, widow of Sir Thomas Rich MP (died in 1803).

[8] Mary Pechell, wife of Brigadier General Caillaud, Commander in Chief, Bengal Army, India.

	formerly Miss Gresham[1]			
	Archdeacon Phillots to Lady Frances Lawrence[2]	—		
November	Mrs Groves		—	

Sir John Eardley-Wilmot 1st Baronet

---

[1] 7th October - Katherine daughter of Sir John Gresham of Titsey Place & wife of William Leveson-Gower.

[2] 15th October - James Phillott (1750-1815), Archdeacon of Bath & 2nd wife Lady Frances St Lawrence, daughter of 1st Earl of Howth. (NB - Jane Austen knew this couple and while writing to her sister, suggested Phillot was only interested in Lady Frances's rank and title, whilst the lady, aged forty-five was so desperate for a husband she was prepared to settle for a widowed clergyman approaching sixty.

1808
Events private.

March	Mr Charles Phillots to another living[1] in Worcestershire.
April	Henry Fanshawe returns to England in the Courageux.
May	Henry Fanshawe is made Commander of the Grasshopper[2] frigate off Cadiz
June	Henry Fanshawe[3] sails in La Belle Ponte to join his own ship.
December	Edward Jenkinson goes on board to accompany the Expedition.

Rev'd Charles Phillots

---

[1] 28th March - appointed Vicar of Badsey and also Wickhamford where he served until his death on 1851. He held several other livings from which he was absent most of the time, leaving a succession of nine curates responsible for the parish. He was also Chaplain to Princess Charlotte, the elder daughter of King George III, when she was Princesss Royal.

[2] 2nd May - Lt. Henry Fanshawe received promotion to Commander with the appointment to command the Grasshopper.

[3] June 1808 - Henry Fanshawe took command of his ship, remaining in the Mediterranean the rest of the year and into 1809.

1808
Events public.

	King of Spain[1] abdicates the Crown in favour of his son.
May	The Prince of the Astorias[2] in compliance with the advice of Bonaparte, restores the crown to father & begs pardon.
	Bonaparte most <u>generously</u> invites the whole Spanish Royal Family to come & live quietly in France, whilst he takes Spain under his protection!
June	Spanish people rise against French oppression in the most spirited manner - send to England for friendship & assistance, proclaim the Prince of Astoria their King - and on the 14 of June the French fleet in Cadiz strike their colours to the Spaniards.
August	Great Spanish & Portuguese successes against the French and the <u>French King of Spain</u>[3] leaves Madrid because <u>the climate disagrees</u> with him
September	Disgraceful convention with Juno by Sir Hew Dalrymple[4] which was the more mortifying by the news being at first understood to relate to unconditional surrender which had been so long

---

[1] Napoleon, attempting to control the Iberian Peninsula, forced the abdication of Charles IV.
[2] Ferdinand VII (1784-1833) reigned briefly in 1808 and again in 1813 until his death.

[3] Joseph, older brother of Napoleon Bonaparte.
[4] Gen. Sir Hew Whiteford Dalrymple, 1st Baronet (1750-1830) a Scottish general in the British Army and Commander of the Portuguese Expedition. Replacing Wellesley he landed on 22nd August after Junot's defeat at Vimiero and immediately halted Wellesley's pursuit of the beaten French to Lisbon. Dalrymple signed a truce on 31st August which permitted Junot to return to France in British ships together with weapons, men and their loot.

	expected by the French to the English Army in Portugal.
November	Trial of Sir Hew Dalrymple owing to the convention[1].
December	Great defeats of the Spanish patriots & the wretch Bonaparte once more triumphs in Madrid.

*Gen. Sir Hew Dalrymple
(1750-1830)*

---

[1] The truce, known as the Convention of Cintra was denounced both in London and Portugal and resulted in Dalrymple being brought home for an enquiry which began 4th October. The result concluded against Dalrymple and consquently he ws never in command on the field again. (N.B. - In 1811 Sir Hew's daughter, Frances Mary Dalrymple married a cousin of AF - Lt. General Edward Fanshawe, a son of Captain Robert Fanshawe, Commissioner of the Plymouth Dockyard).

Published on the 19th January 1808.

'Sunday Reflections very handsomely spoken in July edition of 'The British Critic' & in the 'Gentleman's Magazine' during October'

> 'Sunday Reflections'
> By the Author of Thoughts on Affectations, 8vo.
> 7s. Hatchard. 1809.
>
> 'The pious and sensible Author of this excellent volume, regretting, that although every library abounds with good Sermons, and other religious publications, these are not attainable by servants, has printed these Sunday Reflections for their use and benefit. He has therefore taken the first lessons for the morning and afternoon of each Sunday, as subjects of observation, and has in plain, familiar, but very impressive terms, pointed out and explained the historical facts, and the moral and religious instruction they were severally intended to convey. Nothing can be more modest and unassuming than this Author's opinion of his labours, but there can be no hesitation in recommending these Sunday Reflections as admirably adapted to their purpose. So well indeed do they seem to us to be calculated for servants, and those of humble ranks, who are or may be prevented from attendance at their parish church, that we should be glad to see them printed and circulated in as cheap a form and size as possible. No one can peruse the Reflections on the third Sunday in Lent, p. 113, without being sensible, it is presumed, of the truth and justice of our commendation'.
>
> *(Extract from The British Critic July 1808)*

1809
Family events & circumstances relative to myself.

January 1	Received from Hatchard the 18 copies which are to be my own for the purposes of making presents.
8	A most complemental letter from Mrs Trimmer[1] to whom Hatchard gave a copy.
21	Charles, his wife & two children come to me.
	A most complimentary letter from the Bishop of London[2] about my book of which he supposes him the author.
February 2	I began a fresh medicine for the fits
March 1	Forced to give it up.
7	Begun a different one.
9	Charles & his family leave me.
	Letters of compliment from the Bishop of Durham[3] & the Dean of Canterbury[4]
April 8	Different medicine!
	Charles received a very guarded letter from my brother, the date as far back as Dec. 7th. He does not desire us to write & represents himself as ill & uncomfortable at Petersburgh - only his son William with him, the other two in Finland.

---

[1] Sarah Trimmer (1741-1810) a reformer relating to children's education and literature - possibly the first to consider the history of reading material for children and its access, relativity and impact on young minds. Among her many published books the most popular was 'Fabulous Histories' which came to inspire others to write animal stories for children. As a philanthropist, Trimmer founded Sunday and Charity schools and wrote textbooks and manuals for other ladies who wished to open similar schools. She had important wide connections in the literary world and is considered one of the earliest educational feminists.

[2] Beilby Porteus (1731-1809), Church of England reformer and leading abolitionist and the first senior Anglican to seriously challenge the Church's attitude to slavery.

[3] The Right Rev'd Shute Barrington (1734-1826) last 'Prince Bishop' of Durham.

[4] Thomas Powys (born 1747) appointed Dean of Canterbury in 1797, died 24th November 1809.

June 12	Return to the Mercurial[1] medicine of which Dr Parry has so long had so great an opinion.
August	Second edition of 'Thoughts on Affectation'.
31	Charles comes to me.
September 7	Charles leaves me.
27	Alteration of medicine.
October 10	Receive a very guarded letter from my Brother at Petersburgh, date June 27th - William & Frederic with him.
15	Hear from Charles that he likewise has had a letter from his Father dated the last of August and containing a wild scheme about returning to England. George was then with him
November 12	Charles is taken ill at Warfield of a violent fever from which his life continued in extreme danger till the month of December.
December	When on the 20th he is pronounced out of danger.
	Mr Faithfull[2] comes to Bath & gives a good account of Charles on the whole tho' his recovery must still be a work of a long time.
	My Sister sees a gentleman who saw my Brother at Petersburgh in October uncommonly well & pleasantly situated, his three sons with him.

---

[1] The apothecaries of the 19th and 20th century used many colourful mercurials - calomel, sublimate, cinnober, oxides of mercury and mercury. Calomel pills were used in acute and chronic diseases and also as a diuretic before 'organomercurials' appeared in the 1920s. *ref:The National Center for Biotechnology (USA).*
[2] Revd John Faithfull (1752-1824) Vicar of Warfield, father-in-law of Charles Fanshawe.

1809
Family marriages, deaths or births.

		Marriages	Deaths	Births
February	Mrs White[1], daughter to Commissioner Fanshawe		—	
June	Miss Mary Fanshawe daughter to Commissioner. Fanshawe to the Hon[able] Admiral Robert Stopford[2].	—		
September	Edward Jenkinson[3].		—	
	Mrs Jackson of a girl.[4]			—

Fits 26 - Attacks 293

*Sir Robert Stopford, c.1790-91,
by Henry William Beechey,
National Maritime Museum*

---

[1] Cordelia Fanshawe (1780-1809) - whose widower Admiral Sir John C White KCB later married Charlotte, a daughter of Sir Hew Dalrymple.

[2] Admiral Sir Robert Stopford GCB., GCMG. (1768-1847), a distinguished officer in the Royal Navy whose career spanned more than 60 years.

[3] 28th July - Capt. F. Edwatd Jenkinson, Coldstream Guards was a casualty of the Pennisular Wars, killed in action at the Battle of Talavera, Spain.

[4] 27th Dec (baptism) - Elizabeth Jackson daughter of Revd & Mrs James L Jackson, Rector of Turnerspuddle her married name became Stuart and she died 1885.

1809
Marriages, deaths or Births among acquaintances or neighbours.

		Marriages	Deaths	Births
February	Miss Earle of Swallowfield to the Revd Mr Tindale.[1]	—		
March	Doctor Loveday[2].		—	
April	Miss Scott daughter of Sir William Scott to Mr Townshend.	—		
	Revd Mr C Phillots[3] to Miss Pender	—		
	Doctor Pitcain[4]		—	
	Mr Powys[5] unfortunately missed his way in the dark & was drowned in a pond while walking from the Oxford Road to (Fawley). He had been to attend the Quarter Sessions at Oxford & got out of the chaise in which he was returning with a person going on to (Henley) at Abbington.		—	

---

[1] 22nd February - Mary Anne Earle (1774-1826), daughter of Timothy Hare Earle of Swallowfield Berkshire married Rev. George Thomas Tyndale.

[2] 4th March - John Loveday (1742-1809), married his ward, Anne the heiress of William Taylor Loder of Williamscote. He assisted Richard Chandler in the preparation of the index to the Arundel Marbles - *Marmora Oxoniensia*, (1763) and contributed papers on local antiquities to the *Gentleman's Magazine*.

[3] 6th April - Marriage to Frances Dorothy Pender at Calne, Wilts.

[4] David Pitcairn M.D. FRS (1749-1809), Scottish physician who practised at St Bartholomew's Hospital London, was the first to discover that valvular disease of the heart was frequently caused by rheumatic fever.

[5] Philip Lybbe Powys (1734-1809) of Hardwick House, Oxfordshire.

May	Lady Meredeth.[1]		—
July	Mrs Bracken[2]		—
	Doctor Charles Parry[3] to Miss Bedford	—	
August	Mrs H Isted[4]		—
	Sir George Colebrooke[5]		—
	Sir William Jerningham[6]		—
September	Lady Scott [7] Apoplectic seizure		—
	Miss Vernon[8] daughter of Lord Vernon to Mr Harbord, son to Lord Tuffield	—	
October	Dr Powys, Dean of Canterbury[9]		—

---

[1] 6th May - Mary Gorges Marydith - buried at St Swithin's Church, Bath.

[2] Widow of Revd Thomas Braken of Greenwich.

[3] Charles Parry - eldest son of AF's doctor who as a student accompanied the poet Samuel Taylor Coleridge on a journey to the Harz Mountains. On qualifying he practiced medicine at Bath General Hospital until 1822 when he retired to Brighton to write a wide range of books and translated others from German. In 1825 he published a collection of his father's Medical Writings.

[4] 20th July - Harriet Isted (1753-1809) daughter of Ambrose Isted of Ecton, Northants.

[5] Sir George Colebrooke (1729-1809) - merchant banker & MP for Arundel who while Chairman of the East India Company (1767-1772) made risky speculations and was bankrupt in the crisis of 1772. He retired to Bath and near the end of his life, having paid off his creditors, became a prominent philanthropist.

[6] William Jerningham 6th Bt of Cossey (1736-1809).

[7] 4th September - Anna Maria, wife of Sir William Scott of Doctor's Commons & Erleigh Court and MP for Oxford University 1801-1821.

[8] 19th September - Hon. Georgiana Venables-Vernon, daughter of George, 2nd Lord Vernon of Kinderton, married Edward Harbord, 3rd Baron Suffield.

[9] Rev'd Thomas Powys (1747-1809) - the brother of Mr Philip Lybbe Powys who died in April of the same year.

Mrs Janetta Heathcote[1]	—	
Mrs Hayward[2]	—	

Slovenliness

…certainly a very common, though very odious failing…how often a low servant describes his master's supposed wisdom by what he considers the height of commendation - an assurance that *"He never thinks of such matters, as he his above such stuff!"* And that praise, however mean, is still grateful to numbers of people, must I fear be owned, when we reluctantly reflect how many great and wise men have been known to practise habits, which they were conscious must be disagreeable to others in company, merely to attract attention; and how often apparent neglect of the decencies of custom is put on, as an implication of a mind employed on some abstruse meditation, when its sole aim, after all, was only to call forth what through pretended absence was heard with delight - a remark of that being *always his way!*… AF

---

[1] 17th October - Janetta Heathcote (1737-1809) daughter of William Heathcote.
[2] 22nd December - Anne Hayward, buried at St Swithin's Church, Bath.

1809
Events private.

January	Edward Jenkinson sails
February	The Col[l], Mrs Jenkinson & six daughters come to an house in Northampton Street, Bath which they have hired for eight weeks.
May	The Jenkinsons quit Bath for Coombe.
June	Althea Jenkinson[1] returns to Bath to stay at Mrs Hopton's[2] for the purpose of receiving lessons from Mr Field[3] the Music Master.
July	Henry Jenkinson to go on board the Venerable. Capt Sir Holme Popham to join the present expedition when he is to be changed into Capt. Paget's ship.
	Althea Jenkinson quits Bath & is but in London at Mr Rawlings[4] by her brothers.
August	Death of my ever lamented Browne.
	Edward Jenkinson[5] wounded at Talavera.
September	Henry Jenkinson arrives from Flushing in the Venerable & safe from the illness prevailing in Walcheseum.
	News of Edward Jenkinson's death in consequence of the wound which occasioned the limb to be taken off

---

[1] Althea Jane, daughter of John Jenkinson & Frances Fanshawe (1793-1830).
[2] See 1821 entry by AF: *'Mrs Hopton was the daughter of my father's sister Elisabeth, & the widow of three husbands - Albert, Hale & Hopton'*.
[3] Probably Robert Field who was from a Dublin musical family - in this period his son John Field was composing and performing to considerable acclaim in St Peterburgh.
[4] Possibly Robert Rawlings or his brother James Henry Rawlings musicians of the King's Band - living at 15 Paddington Street.
[5] Lt. Edward Jenkinson 2nd Foot Regiment, The Coldstreams - confirmed killed at the Battle of Televera in 1809 by regimental records. Records of birth not traced but must be assumed as an 'elder' son of John & Frances Jenkinson and named after his father's brother.

	before he was released from his suffering.
	Henry Jenkinson sails again for Flushing in the Venerable.
November	Jenkinsons take a house for the winter at Kensington.
December	Henry Jenkinson returns to England & is made a Lieutenant.
	John Fraser is expelled from Hertford College[1] for the riots in October & by that means loses his writership to the East Indies.

Hertford College - East India Co.

---

[1] Haileybury School - founded in 1806 and originally based at Hertford Castle was used by the East India Company as a training establishment for colonial service. An account of the riots, with details of the consequences was published in a letter dated 8th November 1809 by William Baker (1743-1824)…*"There has been a most scandalous riot at the new East India College, in consequence of which several will be expelled. I have not escaped in the general want of discipline and I have been under the necessity of proceeding against three of the students who have intruded upon our premises in a shameful manner, by shooting at pheasants and wounding others immediately under our garden wall. In the Birch Walk and the other plantations. Two of them were convicted on Saturday last and will be obliged to pay a penalty of £20 each. Besides the tax which they have defrauded - the third having been sent home on the dispersion of the College in consequence of the other more serious riots has not yet appeared, but will be had up in a few days and incur the same penalty. It is to be hoped that the new regulations which the Court of Directors will adopt will prevent this establishment from becoming a public nuisance in the neighbourhood".*

1809
Events public.

January	Death of Sir John Moore[1] in endeavouring to protect the embankment of the English troops from the French forces - the part of the army who are retained in a most harassed condition.
February	Enquiry in the House of Commons into the conduct of the Duke of York[2] - as Commander in Chief.
March	After a long examination of witnesses before a committee of the whole House, the Duke is pronounced not guilty of either participation or connivance in regard to the inquiry which is proved to have been committed by the sale of places - The Duke tho' cleared <u>voluntarily</u> resigned his situation.
April	A great Naval victory[3] over the French by Lords Gambier & Cochrane.
May	A great victory over the French by the Austrians under Arch Duke Charles[4]
July	A great defeat of the Austrian Army[5] by the victorious Bonaparte. Sir Arthur Wellesley's great victory at Talavera[6] Spain over the French.
August	The island of Walcheum taken[7]

---

[1] Lt. Gen. Sir John Moore, KB (1761-1809) - known as 'Moore of Corunna' following his death during the Peninsular War at the Battle of Corunna where he repulsed the French army under Marshal Soult. He is also noted for military training reforms.

[2] The enquiry into 'commissions granted' had discovered the Duke's mistress was responsible for adding names to lists without the Duke being aware.

[3] 11th - 24th April - Battle of the Basque Roads.

[4] 21st - 22nd May - Battle of Aspern-Essling.

[5] 5th - 6th July - Battle of Wagram.

[6] 27th - 28th July - Battle of Talavera, Sir Arthur Wellesley's first great victory of the Peninsular War.

[7] While attempting to seal the port of Antwerp and destroy the French fleet, the British seized the swampy island of Walcheren at the mouth of the river Scheldt.

September	~~The victorious expedition to return because unable to proceed!!~~
	Duel between two of the Prime Ministers[1] - Lord Castlereagh & Mr Canning - the token wound ended.
October 25	The fiftieth[2] year of the King's reign - kept a general Jubilee all over the kingdom.
December	Peace between France & Austria.
	Walcheren is evacuated & the expedition over as last really return.
	Bonaparte repudiates[3] his <u>beloved</u> Empress because she brings him no children.

The Divorce of the Empress Josephine (1809)
- Henri Frederic Schopin

The occupying troops soon began to suffer a combination of malaria, typhus and dysentery and within a month 8,000 cases of 'Walcheren Fever' were reported.

[1] 21st September 1809 Foreign Secretary, George Canning who disputed with Lord Castlereagh, Secretary of State for War and the Colonies, on finding the troops he wanted to deploy to Portugal had already been sent to the Netherlands by Castlereagh. Canning threatened to resign unless Castlereagh was removed and convinced Prime Minister Portland to secretly agree to make the change as soon as possible. When Castlereagh discovered the plan he challenged Canning to a duel on Putney Heath. As Canning, had never previously fired a pistol he consequently missed, while Castlereagh, one of the best shots of his generation, wounded Canning in the thigh.

[2] King George III - third longest reigning British monarch (1760-1820).

[3] 10th January - Napoleon divorced Joséphine.

1810
Family events & circumstances relative to myself alone.

January	Hatchard writes me word of the Queen, Princess Elizabeth first, & then others sent & Princess Augusta having sent for several copies of 'Sunday Reflections'.
February 14	Little Charles Fanshawe taken so ill as to prevent his father coming to Bath, mends in about a week when …
March 1	Charles comes to me.
	Charles has received a most extraordinary letter from his Father - date Dec. 24th amplifying of the strongest discontent yet clearly showing that he has brought all his difficulties entirely upon himself & by his madness of vanity seems to me in the way to ruin, his sons also - in case leaving is in order; to live in the country with his friend Princess Branicka[1].
17	Charles leaves Bath.
April	Strange letters from my Brother having at some changes in his situation but not explaining what.
April 26	Alteration of medicine
	Alter again.
May 3	Charles comes from Dengie to Kensington to marry his Brother to his cousin Anna Maria *[Jenkinson]*
X May 6	By my Sister's means, sent a packet of letters to my Brother accompanied by the miniature of his late wife which he knows I have.

---

[1] Aleksandra Branicka, (1754-1838), known as Saneckka and Countess Branicka was a niece and confidante of Potemkin and the favourite lady-in-waiting of Catherine the Great. Due to her importance in the Imperial Court she was treated as a member of the Imperial family. Via her marriage to Branicki she administered vast estates in the Ukraine.

August 19	Charles receives a <u>mighty mysterious</u> letter from his Father, as much addressed to his brother Henry as to himself, in which he confirms his intention of allowing him the promised £400 per ann. on his marriage, but again speaks of the foolish plan of sending his two youngest sons to England.
25	My Sister receives a letter from my Brother acknowledging the receipt of the miniature & is trying sea bathing for his health - date July 18th.
	Illness independent of the fits occasions great alteration of medicine.
September	Return to old ways.
20	Little Charles Fanshawe fractures his skull & undergoes the operation of Trepanning[1]
October	Another Royal order for books
December	Charles hears again from his Father with re-mention of the English plan for his sons.
	Charles carries the poor little boy to London for advice - the case pronounced a complete one - yet the head requires support.
28	A letter from my brother or rather a packet for it contains letters to my Sister to Charles & his brother jointly, to Lord Whitworth[2], Lord Malgrave[3], Dr

---

[1] A surgical intervention performed since ancient times when a hole is drilled or scraped into the human skull until the perforation exposes the *dura mater*. This allows treatment to intracranial diseases and releases pressure by blood buildup from an injury - which might have applied to the case of this small boy.

[2] Charles Whitworth, 1st Earl Whitworth, GCB, PC (1752-1825) envoy-extraordinary and minister-plenipotentiary at St. Petersburg,(1789-1801).

[3] General Henry Phipps, 1st Earl of Mulgrave, GCB, PC (1755-1831) Foreign Secretary under William Pitt the Younger (1805-1806).

> Bentham[1], Mr Yorke[2] & to myself - but the date of mine being as far back as June & besides being mysterious & romantic in the highest degree - it is completely unintelligible in that to Charles he speaks of being going to pass his Winter in Poland & his Spring in his lands.

Beauty

Affectation of beauty so regularly excites the unbounded ridicule, that it is astonishing to see how continually it is practised by the old, the ugly and even by the most deformed people of both sexes; whose glasses, those never-neglected monitors, so honestly reflect what none but the self-beholder views with eyes of admiration…Let us rather be satisfied with the appearance it has pleased God to give us. We may injure, but shall not mend his works! If we are ugly, let us no otherwise attempt to adorn that ugliness, than by an endeavour at a constant exercise of good-nature and benevolence, which infuses a pleasing cheerfulness into the least agreeable set of features, and lights up even an ugly countenance with more attraction than can be purchased in all the shops of the metropolis!... AF

---

[1] Jeremy Bentham 1748-1832) philosopher, jurist, social reformer and polymath who travelled in Russia during 1786/7 visiting his brother Samuel and engaged in managing industrial and other projects for Prince Potemkin.

[2] Probably Charles Philip Yorke MP (1764-1834) Secretary of War (1801/3) and other ministerial appointments which included 1st Lord of the Admiralty (1801-12).

1810
Family marriages, deaths or births.

		Marriages	Deaths	Births
February 14	Mrs Boisragon[1] a boy.			—
	Mrs C Fanshawe a boy John[2].			—
April	Frederic Wollaston[3] died at St. Kitts last September.		—	
May 3	Henry Fanshawe to Anna Maria Jenkinson.[4]	—		
June 11	Sophia Wollaston[5].		—	
December	Mrs Haggitt[6] - daughter of Commissioner Fanshawe.		—	
	Mrs Jackson a boy[7].			—

Fits 26 - Attacks 123

---

[1] 6th February - Theodore Smith Gurenstone Boisragon son of Henry Boisragon & Mary Annetta Fanshawe, the only daughter of John Gascoyne Fanshawe of Parsloes (AF's 3rd cousin once removed).

[2] 18th March - John Faithfull Fanshawe.

[3] Frederick Hyde Wollaston (1770-1809) - was connected to the family of Drewry Ottley of St Vincent, West Indies.

[4] Marriage of 1st cousins - AF's nephew Henry Fanshawe & neice Anna Maria Jenkinson.

[5] Sophia Hyde Wollaston (1777-1810) daughter of Rev'd Francis Wollaston astronomer & FRS.

[6] Christiana (1771-1810), daughter of Capt. Robert Fanshawe RN, Commissioner of Plymouth Dockyard & M.P - who in 1776 married Revd Francis Haggitt, Rector of Nuneham Courtenay, Oxford.

[7] 26th December (baptism) Robert Leonard, son of Revd James l Jackson & Louisa Decima Wollaston.

1810
Marriages, deaths or Births among acquaintances or neighbours.

		Marriages	Deaths	Births
April	Lady Talbot[1]		—	
	Mrs Tho. Powys - three children[2]			—
May	Mr Lloyd[3] formerly of Silchester		—	
June	At Blount's house which they had long left, our neighbours Lady Price		—	
	Mrs Loten[4]		—	
	Mr John Roper to Miss Pott[5]	—		
July	Mr Bowen to Miss Boycott[6]	—		
August	Mrs Evans[7] of Brock Street		—	
December	Miss Bowdler[8], niece to my friend Mrs H Bowdler		—	

---

[1] 21st August - Rt. Hon Elizabeth Talbot, Dowager Countess of Shrewsbury buried at Bath Abbey.

[2] 15th November (Baptism) of triplets James, Philip & Letitia Powys born at Fawley.

[3] Revd Eusebius Lloyd of Silchster Hants.

[4] 11th June - Lettice (Cotes) Loten (1733-1810) wife of Johannes Gideon Loten (1710-1789) of the Dutch East India Co & 29th Governor of Zeylan, Fellow of the Royal Society & Fellow of the Society of Antiquaries of London.

[5] 13th June - John Bonfoy Roper of Berkhampstead Castle, MP for Huntingdonshire, married Harriet Pott at Marylebone.

[6] *Extract from the Piozzi Letters: 1805-1810)* - 'And do you remember Sophia Boycott her sister, a very tall large showy woman? She is married to Bowen, the Apothacary!!...Bowen's purse is rated at £100,000'.

[7] 9th August - Catherine (Coker) Evans (1746-1810) wife of Revd Arthur Evans (1735-1789).

[8] 4th December - Elizabeth Bowdler, daughter of Thomas Bowdler the Younger.

1810
Events private.

January	Henry Fanshawe goes on board the Clyde[1] - Capt. Owen.
February	Henry Jenkinson sailed on the 2nd for Portugal
	Capt. Stewart instead of Owen who is detained on the Walcheren Inquiry.
March	Henry Fanshawe returns to England being sent with despatches, & goes to Kensington on a visit.
April	Henry Jenkinson returns to England in the Clyde.
	The family of the Boissier quit Bath for ever. Sell their house and have taken one in the country.
May	Capt. & Mrs Fanshawe go to Portsmouth to serve there till the Grasshopper is ready for sea. Fanny Jenkinson goes to Portsmouth to remain with her sister till the Captain goes to sea.
June	Henry Jenkinson sails in the Clyde for the coast of Africa.
	Henry Fanshawe sails in the Grasshopper as a convoy for Nova Scotia
	Poor old Jaynes leaves Bath for ever.
	Mrs Fanshawe returns to the Jenkinsons with whom she is to remain during her husband's absence.
August	The destination of the Clyde was changed & H.J. returns to England and is at Deal.
	Henry Jenkinson sails again.
September	C.S.F Fanshawe fractures his skull & is trepanned.
October	Henry Fanshawe returns from America & Mrs Fanshawe goes to him at Deal.
November	Col¹ Jenkinson takes a house at Kensington for the

[1] On 6 February 1810 *Clyde* was under the command of Captain John Stuart when, after a five-hour chase, she captured the French privateer lugger *Transit*, of 14 guns and 45 men.

	winter.
December	Dr Wollaston has £1000 left him by an old neighbour, a Mrs [Jove]
	Henry Jenkinson sails in the Inconstant[1] for Vera Cruz..
	Mrs Fanshawe to stay at her Father's during her husband's absence - who is now at Portsmouth.

Indulgence for the failings of others

'...Sincere indulgence for the failings of others by no means requires the blindness to the faults of those we love, which is sometimes observable in people of warm affections and not very strong understandings. But as a blind person cannot judge of objects of sight, so blind love, or silly laughing good-nature, cannot be indulgent to error of which it is in fact ignorant. To be truly indulgent, there must first be a strong perception of error....' AF

---

[1] Inconstant underwent a refit in 1810 at Portsmouth and sailed from December that year under the command of Captain Edward Owen (later Admiral Sir Edward Owen).

1810
Events public.

	Walcheren Enquiry
March	Capture of the Island of Guadaloupe.
	Bonaparte marries the Archduchess Lousia Maria of Austria[1].
April	Sir Francis Burdett[2] committed to the Tower in consequence of a most inflametory pamphlet reflecting on the King & the conduct of Ministry - refuses to retract - in consequence of which, there are for three days riots in London & he is on the 9th day of the month conveyed forcibly to the Tower with a strong military guard.
May	Riots in Bath by the less kind of local philistines but put a stop to by the arrival of troops from Bristol who are sent for to keep the peace.
	An attempt to murder the Duke of Cumberland[3] who is terribly wounded by an Italian servant named Sellis who on finding himself unable to succeed in his villainous attempt 'cos the Duke who waked from the

---

[1] 1st April - Marie Louise (1791-1847), Austrian archduchess, 2nd wife of Napoleon, known as Empress of the French and Queen of Italy then after his abdication, Duchess of Parma.

[2] Sir Francis Burdett, 5th Bt., MP (1770-1844) argued for policital reform and in 1810 denounced the actiions of Parliament by questioning the power to imprison a radical named John Gale - a revised edition of his speech was then published in the Weekly Register and as a result he spent a short period in the Tower, however some of the reforms he advocated were eventually incorporated in the 1832 Reform Act. His wife being a daughter of the banker Thomas Coutts, resulted in their daughter Angela Burdett Coutts inheriting her grandfather's fortune when she became known as a major philanthropist.

[3] 31st May - The Duke of Cumberland, 5th son of George III experienced this attempt on his life at St James' Palace. It was widely reported and The Times carried the personal testimony of the Duke. At the time there was wide speculation about the true facts which are still debated even today.

	blows called for help' - retired to his own room & was found with his throat cut by himself with a razor & was heard struggling when the Duke called at his door for his assistance!
	Death of Mr Windham[1].
September	Surrender of Almeida[2] to the Franch troops.
October	Victory over the French troops in Portugal
	Capture of the Isle de Bourbon[3].
November	Death of the Princess Amelia[4]
	The King is seized with the terrible malady with which he has before been afflicted!
December	Death of Mrs Trimmer[5]
	The King in great danger from a fever & bowel complaint.

---

[1] 4th June - William Windham PC (1750-1810) of Felbrigg Hall, Norfolk was a Whig politician and outstanding orator who counted among his many friends Charles James Fox and Edmund Burke.

[2] 26th August - Almeida, a border garrison fortress between Spain & Portugal was captured by the French under Marshal Michel Ney after having beseiged the forces of Brig. Gen. William Cox.

[3] The surrender of Isle de France (Mauritius) & Isle de Bourbon (Reunion) marked the capture of the last French territory east of Africa.

[4] 2nd November - HRH Princess Amelia (1783-1810), the youngest child of King George III.

[5] 15th December - Sarah Trimmer (1741-1810) writer and critic of British children's literature and an educational reformer. Her periodical 'The Guardian of Education' reviewed children's literature seriously for the first time. She created the first history of children's literature and also 'Fabulous Histories', her most popular children's book which remained in print for more than a century. She inspired numerous other animal stories for children. Mrs Trimmer founded several Sunday and charity schools and wrote textbooks and manuals to equip other women to start their own schools.

1811
Family events & circumstances relative to myself.

February 13	Ill with a pain & swelling in my right foot.
19	Decided to be the gout - am completely lame and wrapped up in costume!
March 14	Return to my own shoe & stocking. Began a new medicine in the form of hops.
April 1	Seized with a fit in the Crescent, carried by Dr. Bowen into Mrs Gwynne's house & then brought home in a chair.
27	Charles, Mrs C & the eldest boy come to me.
May 11	Deliver all papers belonging to or concerning my brother to Charles as his father's attorney.
17	Charles & his family leave me.
19	Alteration of medicine - am cupped[1] for my headaches - without much effect.
July	A new <u>very strong</u> cordial seems to do me some degree of good, for I walk with less disturb.
August 2	A letter from my Brother gives notice of him [hearing that] with my <u>'Easter Holidays'</u>, read and understood by one of the daughters of Prince Pomiatowski[2] at Jagaashky near Kiev in the banks of the Daieper, from whence he dates his letter March 22
August 6	Taken extremely ill, as in the old way & as I believe in considerable danger but by Dr Parry's constant attention & skill, on the 22nd was able to walk out

---

[1] Medical technique - small 'cups' are applied to the skin creating a vacumn which draws blood vessels to the cupped area.
[2] Prince Józef Antoni Poniatowski (1763-1813), a nephew of King Stanislaus Augustus of Poland was a Polish general and Minister of War and Marshal of the French Empire during the Napoleonic Wars.

	for a few minutes.
September 1	A fit in the old way, tho' remarkably bad & after it, recover surprisingly - the cordial to which I returned some time ago seems to agree wonderfully.
	Paid my landlord Mr Thomas Langley of Borough Farm, Surrey who is executor to my late landlord Mr Pennicott - £2150 for the house I have purchased off him in Brock Street.
25	Make a fresh Will leaving house & everything to Charles - witnessed by Mrs Bowdler, Mr [Spezal], Mr Tull[1] - one copy in Dr Parry's keeping, the other in my small square box.
November	Dr Parry begins a new plan of <u>very</u> frequent leaching.
December	Insured plate furniture - at the Globe[2] Insurance Office, Pall Mall & Cornhill - Nr. of policy 46326.
2	Fit in the Crescent, carried into Mr Daubery's house - home in a chair.

Brook Street, Bath

---

[1] Possibly of the family of Ebenezar Tull of Gay Street.
[2] The Globe Insurance Co. established in 1803 specialised in fire & life insurance. Operating in Pall Mall and Cornhill, the latter premises at the Bank junction were continually used until late 20th century by the Royal Insurance Group with which the Globe had merged.

1811
Family marriages, deaths or births.

		Marriages	Deaths	Births
February	Miss C Hyde to the Revd Robert Walpole[1]	—		
April	Mrs Fanshawe of Parsloes[2]		—	
May	Col. Duckworth[3] killed at Albuhera in Portugal		—	
June	Capt. Ed. Fanshawe[4] to Major H Dalrymple's daughter	—		
July 16	Mrs C Fanshawe of a daughter Ellen[5].			—

[Numbers of Fits & Attacks were not recorded]

---

[1] 6th February - Caroline Francis Hyde married Rev'd Robert Walpole (1781-1856). Rector at Christ Church, Marylebone, London - a classical scholar, and great-nephew of Sir Robert Walpole the 18th century statesman.

[2] 22nd March - Mary Parkinson (1747-1811) widow of John Gascoyne Fanshawe of Parsloes (1746-1803).

[3] 16th May - Lt. Col. George H Duckworth of the 48th Regiment of Foot - killed in action at Albeura, - husband of Penelope Fanshawe.

[4] 15th June - Lt Gen. Edward Fanshawe C.B (1785-1858) son of Capt. Robert Fanshawe Commissioner of the Plymouth Dockyard, married Frances Mary Dalrymple (1790-1865) daughter of Gen. Sir Hew Dalrymple.

[5] 30th August (baptism) - Ellen Faithfull Fanshawe.

1811

Marriages, deaths or Births among acquaintances or neighbours.

		Marriages	Deaths	Births
January	Mrs Rich of Swincombe		—	
	Mrs Pott[1]		—	
April	Mrs Jane Davies[2]		—	
	Major Hatsell[3] of Green Park Place		—	
June	Mrs C Parry a girl[4]			—
July	Mr Reynolds[5] of the Crescent		—	
	Sir Wm Young[6]		—	
	Mr Fawkener[7] - son of Sir Everard[8] & Lady Fawkener - afterwards married to Governor Powall - suddenly in the Circus.		—	

---

[1] 18th January - Sarah Elizabeth (Cruttenden) Pott (1723-1811), wife of Sir Percival Pott of St Bart's Hospital, London, who was an important influence on medicine and the modern understanding of diseases - his name is memorialised by Pott's fracture, Pott's disease of the spine, and Pott's puffy tumor. He was also the first to recognise the occupational association between carcinoma and chimney sweeps.

[2] 15th April - Jane Davies (1741-1811) buried in Bath Abbey.

[3] 20th April - William Hatsell (1737-1811).

[4] 2nd August - Emma Gertrude Parry the first child of Charles, eldest son of Dr. Parry.

[5] 27th July - Edmund Reynolds - retired West India planter.

[6] Sir William Young, Governor of Tobago who died in the West Indies.

[7] William Augustus Fawkener (1750-1811), who in 1791 when a clerk to the Privy Council, was sent on a secret mission to Empress Catherine II of Russia. He is kown to have been a friend of James Boswell.

[8] Everard Fawkener (1684-1758), a silk merchant, secretary to the Duke of Cumberland who also held posts as Ambassador to Turkey, and Postmaster General. Of special interest is his relationship with the philosopher Voltaire who mainly stayed at Fawkener's home whenever he viited England.

September	Dr Raine[1] of the Charter House		—	
	Mrs William Tangmir		—	
October	Dr Reynolds[2]		—	
	Mrs M Smith of Swincombe		—	
November	Mr L Tassier[3] (whom I knew at Naples)		—	
	Mrs Senior[4] of Brock Street.		—	

The Circus, Bath

---

[1] 17th September - Dr Matthew Raine (1760-1811) Headmaster of Charterhouse School from 1791 - buried at The Charterhouse.
[2] Henry Revell Reynolds (1745-1811) physician to King George III.
[3] Louis (Lewis) Tessier (c1736-1811) a silk merchant & son of a Huguenot refugee.
[4] 10th November - Charlotte Senior, a widow aged 73, buried at Bath Abbey.

1811
Events private.

February	Capt Fane[1] taken prisoner in xxxxx Palamós his ship the Cambrian[2]
	Mrs Fanshawe goes to her husband who returns to Portsmouth & is forced to leave her in three days after their meeting.
March	Captain Fanshawe returns again till further orders - goes again in three days.

Elegance of manner and of dress

'...There was a time, not very many years ago, when *some* distinction of dress was observable in different classes; I may now without exaggeration affirm that there is *none*. For though the wife of a peer will always be known from that of a butcher, and a housemaid from her mistress, by the manner of wearing and of putting it on; yet in form of the clothing, and even in the materials of which it is composed, there is now but little difference. The vanity of *equality* of dress is a luxury of increasing growth in the nation, which will in a few years be but too severely felt by the light=hearted young people of the present hour; who thoughtlessly enjoy the extreme similarity of apparel, which makes it, in a place of public resort, a point requiring consideration to know a lady from her servant...' AF

---

[1] Francis Fane (1778-1844) later Rr. Admiral - younger son of John Fane & Lady Elizabeth Parker, daughter of 3rd Earl of Macclesfield.

[2] The Cambrian with the Kent and Ajax attacked Palamós, southern Spain - the landing party destroying six merchant vessels with supplies for the French army. Although successful 33 British men were killed, 89 wounded, 86 taken prisoner and 1 deserted. The Cambrian lost one man only but seven were wounded and four missing, including Fane who was taken prisoner where he remained for the rest of the war.

	After a third return he sails for Guernsey & Mrs F accompanies him - strikes on a wind force off the Isle of Wight & puts in at Cowes to repair.
April	Mrs Fanshawe at Jersey where she is to remain all the summer whilst her husband comes on the French coast & is occasionally with him.
May	Mr Young carried to London by a medical man owing to insanity under which he has laboured for some months.
	Both Fanny & Sophia Jenkinson gone & are to stay with Mrs F[1] at Jersey.
	Jenkinsons give up the house at Kensington & remove to Coombe.
June	Col. Jenkinson promoted to the rank of Major General.
	Mrs Fanshawe & her Sisters come from Jersey for the Grasshopper to refit at Portsmouth
July	Henry Jenkinson returns from Vera Cruz with the Inconstant - has had the yellow fever[2] but is well - sails again.
	Mrs F to return to the General & then go again to remain at Sheerness till the Grasshopper sails.
25	Henry sails & Mrs F goes to Dengie.
September 8	A letter from my Brother to my Sister dated July 19th giving notice of his sons William & George being admitted again into the Russian service in the Emporer's own Regiment of Simionovski Foot Guards[3] - William as a Lieutenant and George as an Ensign.
August	Gen. Jenkinson is presented with a Silver Cup value

---

[1] Their sister Anna Dora, wife of their cousin Henry Fanshawe.
[2] Yellow fever - a disease transmitted by infected mosquitos.
[3] Garrisoned at St. Petersburgh - one of the two oldest guards regiments in the Imperial Russian Army.

	£100 by the officers of those regiments he inspected during the inspectorship which he loses in consequence of his increased rank.	
	Mr Young returns home and is considered as well.	
September	Capt. Fane[1] returns to Wormsley.	
	Gen. Jenkinson, my Sister & Fanny go on a tour & take Shiplake[2] in their way where they go to church - attempts to see Shiplake Hill where they are refused admittance but are told that this is on sale.	
October	A letter from Henry to his wife gives notice of his having seen his father & his Brothers at Reval[3] whither they came from Petersburgh to see him, in consequence of his having written to give notice of the chance - he hopes to be home in November but te business on which he went has completely failed.	
November	Mr Phillott[4] the Surgeon chosen to be Mayor of Bath.	
	Shiplake Hill bought for 7000 Guineas by Lord Mark Kerr[5], a Naval Officer, son of the late Marquis of Lothian.	
December	Jenkinsons remove from Coombe Cottage to Kensington for the winter.	
	Henry Jenkinson passes nearly three weeks with his family & then returns to his ship.	

---

[1] Captain Francis Fane returned to the home of his parents at Wormsley.
[2] In 1760 AF's father took up the tenancy of Whitehouse, Shiplake near Henley-on Thames where the family remained until 1803 - there friendships were formed with the family of Thomas Parker, 4th Earl of Macclesfield.
[3] Port in the Baltic - now known as Tallinn, Estonia.
[4] Joseph Phillott (1782-1833) Surgeon at Bath General Hospital.
[5] Vice-Admiral Lord Mark Robert Kerr (1776-1840), an Royal Navy officer and 3rd son of 5th Marquess of Lothian. He married 3rd daughter of 6th Earl, and Marquess of Antrim, succeding him as Countess of Antrim in her own right upon the death of her elder sister.

Lord Mark Kerr

1811
Events public.

February	The Prince of Wales to act as Regent during the King's illness.
	The Isle of France[1] & Banda[2] taken from the French.
March	Great victory of the French at Cadiz under General Graham - called Battle of Barrossa[3].
	The French army in Portugal retreat before Lord Wellington.
May	The King somewhat better but relapses before the end of the month.
	Great victory over the French at Albuara in Portugal. Marshal Berresford against Marshall Soutt.[4]
September	The King whose life had been despaired of recovers some degree of bodily but none of mental health.
November	A comet[5] makes its appearance.
September	Dreadful fire[6] at Greenwich Hospital with the loss however of only one life.
November	The King very ill again.

---

[1] Mauritius in the Indian Ocean, from 1715 a French Colony.

[2] In the Spice Islands, Banda was fought over for centuries as the world's only source of the preserving spices of nutmeg and mace. When in 1810 , the islands in the control of Holland fell to Napoleon - once again Banda became a target for the British.

[3] Battle of Barrosa or Chiclana during the Penisular War was fought 5th March 1811.

[4] Battle of Albuera fought 16th May 1811.

[5] The Great Comet of 1811 (officially - C/1811 F1) was visible to the naked eye for about 260 days - the longest period of visibility on record until the appearance of Comet Hale-Bopp in 1997.

[6] The infirmary for old army pensioners was built early in the reign of George III - was partly destroyed by the fire.

December	Capture of Batava[1] in the Island of Java.
	Horrid murders[2] of Mr & Mrs Marr & their infant child & likewise of a Mr & Mrs Williamson, alehourse keepers - both families living in Ratcliffe Highway. The perpitrators of the crime not yet <u>positively</u> discovered - tho' one who destroys himself to avoid what would have been probably against him seems certainly to have had a hand in the sad tragedy - he is legally buried with the disgrace due to suicide.
	Terrible riots at Nottingham[3].

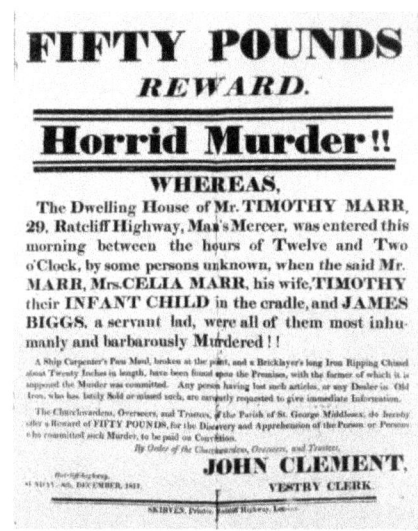

---

[1] Batavia fell on 8th August, and within two months the whole island had been taken.

[2] The Ratcliff Highway Murders - attacks upon the Marr and Williamson families when 7 people were killed. These crimes occurring only 12 days apart took place in December 1811, with both families living within half a mile of each other on Ratcliff Highway (now part of the London Docklands). The main suspect John Williams, committed suicide before trial.

[3] East Midlands Luddite campaign started in 1811, involving gangs of masked men who smashed the machines of the traditional hosiery factories were workers were being exploited.

1812
Family events & circumstances relative to myself.

January 21	Hatchard who has paid for my new scheme 30 cents - my old account.
February 7	Begin a fresh medicine. Hatchard sends my payment.
March 5	Send my manuscript.
20	Receive the first proof.
21	Charles, his wife & eldest boy come to me. The Faithfull[1] family at Bath at the same time, but I am too ill to see them.
25	Walked out for the first time since 2nd of last December.
April 10	Charles & his family leave me.
17	Insured my house from Lady Day[2] at the Globe[3] Insurance Office, Pall Mall & Cornhill - No of Policy 47992.
May 19	Returned my last proof.
June 5	Receive my own 18 copies from Hatchards - price 5/6.
18	Published - <u>Occasional Considerations.</u>
24	Hear from Mr Lane that I am entitled to £90 Stock at 5 p^r ct due to me on my 18 shares of West Jersey Society.
July 24	Messrs Drummonds give me notice & send the Transfer receipt of £90 Stock paid to me in the 3p^r ct consolidated annuities according to Mr Lane's letter.
August 8	Begin a new medicine.

---

[1] Family of Charles Fanshawe's wife Patty.
[2] Legal quarter day - 25th March.
[3] Globe Insurance Office merged in 1864 - as the Liverpool London & Globe Ins Office - and in later mergers absorbed into the Royal & Sun-Alliance Ins Group.

9	A most complmental letter from the B. of Durham[1] on the book - whose great age & character make one proud of the phrase that <u>he</u> hopes for improvement to himself from it!
October 2	Turned with a fit in the Gravel walk & brought home in a chair.
6	Begin a new medicine.
18	...the same rank in the Army & is again going out; his son Frederick to accompany him - William is Aide de Camp to Prince Augustus of Oldenburgh[2], George to General Fowke - the difference of six days from this letter to then received by Charles makes it more than probable that he was not at Moscow at the time of the demolition.
December 1	Begin a new medicine.

Fits 31 - Attacks 152

Rev'd Shute Barrington, Bishop of Durham & Salisbury - Thomas Lawrence

---

[1] Rt. Rev'd Shute Barrington (1734-1826).
[2] Prince Augustus of Oldenburgh (later Grand Duke) left the Duchy of Oldenburgh in December 1810 after annexation by the French Empire and remained in exile with the Russian imperial family. The annexation of Oldenburgh which contributed to the rift between France and Russia and the allies, ended in 1812.

1812
Family marriages, deaths or births.

		Marriages	Deaths	Births
February	Miss Louisa Rivers to Mr Story[1]	—		
May	Sir Henry Rivers to Miss Eales[2]	—		
July	Mrs Edward Fanshawe a boy[3]			—
October	Mrs Karslake[4] a boy			—
December	Mrs Freeling[5]		—	

---

[1] 18th February - Louisa Rivers daughter of Rev. Sir Peter Rivers Gay prebendary of Winchester Cathedral married Joseph Story of Bingfield, County Caven, Ireland.

[2] 30th April - Rev'd Sir Henry Rivers (1774-1851) Lord of the Manor of Walcot from 1834 and a member of the clergy, married Charlotte Eales (born 1796).

[3] 3rd July - Robert Dalrymple Fanshawe.

[4] 18th September - birth of William Heberden Karslake at Dolton, Devon.

[5] 26th December (burial) Emilia Henrietta (Rivers) Freeling at Walcot wife of Francis Freeling and sister of [1] (above).

1812
Marriages, deaths or Births among acquaintances or neighbours.

		Marriages	Deaths	Births
February	Lady Charles Spencer[1].		—	
	Mrs Honywood of Brock Street[2].		—	
March	Mrs Fraser[3], widow of the Doctor.		—	
	Miss Fanny Rich of Sonning[4]			
May	Mr Annesley of Reading[5]		—	
	Lady Macclesfield[6]		—	
	Mrs W[il] Heberden[7]		—	
August	Mr Else[8] of Fountains Buildings		—	

---

[1] 13th January - Lady Mary Beauclerk (1743-1812) daughter of Vere Beauclerk, 1st Baron Vere & wife of Lord Charles Spencer a politician and Gentleman of the Bedchamber to George III.

[2] 9th February - Elizabeth, widow of Revd John Honywood, Prebendary of Salisbury & eldest daughter of Revd Dr.Wake, Prebendary of Westminster.

[3] Dr William M Fraser died 1807, former physician extraordinary to George, Prince of Wales.

[4] Frances Rich of Sonning probate granted 29th December 1812.

[5] 17th April - Francis Annesley (1734-1812) MP for Reading 1774-1806.

[6] 20th May - Mary, daughter of Sir William Heathcote & widow of Thomas Parker, 3rd Earl of Macclesfield FRS (1723-1795) politician.

[7] 21st May - Elizabeth (Miller) Heberden, wife of Dr William Heberden the Younger. Her death at 36 had left 9 children motherless which resulted in the admirable Dr. Heberden to sacrifice his brilliant career to raise them. However, he continued to act as 'physician ordinary' to George III and Queen Charlotte at Windsor - and his story is beautifully recorded in the annuals of the Royal College of Physicians praising his reputation as a physician and father.

[8] 11th August - Richard Else (1776-1812) a solicitor practicing in Bath.

October	Baroness Dimsdale[1]	—
November	Sir Charles Talbot[2]	—
	Mrs Streatfield[3]	—
	Mrs Lysaghts[4] of Brock Street	—
	Mr Edward Jerningham[5]	—
December	General Caillaud[6]	—

Thomas Dimsdale.MP
attributed to Nathaniel Plimer
watercolour, 1780's
© National Portrait Gallery, London

[1] 16th October - Elizabeth Dimsdale, 3rd wife of Baron Thomas Dimsdale MP (1712-1800) left an interesting and large published collection of recipes and papers. Her husband a doctor was a leading expert in smallpox inoculation and went by invitation to Russia to innoculate Empress Catherine - and was rewarded with his baronial title and a substantial pension.

[2] 11th November (burial) - Sir Charles Talbot (1751-1812) MP for Weobly 1800-1802, Rye 1803-1806 & for Bletchingley 1812.

[3] 31st October - Lady Anne Sidney (1730-1812), widow of Henry Streatfield (1706-1762) lived at Penhurst - the only child of Jocelyn Sidney, 7th Earl of Leicester whose title became extinct on his death.

[4] 19th November - Ann Lysaght - a daughter of Henry Wrixon of Glinhill, Cork.

[5] 17th November - Edward Jerningham (1737-1812) - a poet in the circle of Chesterfield, Walpole & Sheridan, who was a confident of George, The Prince Regent.

[6] Brigadier-General John Caillaud (1726-1812) Commander-in-Chief, India - retired 1775.

1812
Events Private.

January	Heard of the misfortune of the Grasshopper being seized by the Dutch after a vicious storm which she had weathered & with all her crew carried prisoners into the Texel[1]. Henry Fanshawe however writes in good spirits to his wife, rejoicing having escaped with life - he saw the Hero, a 74 sank & eight ships of the convoy were lost!
February 25	Henry Fanshawe certainly now at Verdun, a draft being now come over from him dated from thence on the 8th of this month.
April	Anna receives a few lines from H F from Verdun where he is in daily expectation of her joining him.
	Charles receives a letter from his brother George dated Jan 30th Petersburgh, in which he speaks of his father as still in Poland.
	Anna[2] sails for [Morlaix][3] in the Peter & John, Capt. Ferris on the 15th from Plymouth.
25	Hear of the return of the Castel bringing a letter written before she landed.
May	Hear of her again, got as far as Paris.
	A letter from my Brother addressed to the whole family dated from Countess Branicka in Poland, Jan. 27th - he has heard of H F's misfortune.

---

[1] Christmas Day 1811 - the Island of Texel belonged to Holland, at war with Britain. HMS Grasshopper, caught on the perilous Haak Sands rode out a terrific storm and could only watch helplessly as HMS Hero at a distance of mile, was destroyed with the loss of more than 500 men.The details of this event are available as a result of Henry Fanshawe's evidence at his court-martial in 1814, where he wase absolved of any blame for the loss of his ship to the enemy.

[2] Anna Maria (Jenkinson) Fanshawe attempts to join her husband, P.O.W at Verdun.

[3] Possibly Morlaix, Brittany, France.

June 13	Henry Jenkinson removed from the Inconstant to the 'Impetuna' Admiral Marttins Jilaz' ship off Lisbon whither he sails with him to Acasto on the -
	My Sister has received a letter from Mrs Fanshawe arrived safely at Verdun- May 7th
	Another letter from my Brother to Charles, still in Poland dated April 3
July	Another letter to Charles dated June 10th.
August	Another letter from my Brother, June 24th from Petersburgh - speaking with hope that the present change of affairs may bring him again into employment - his sons George & William are with the army & Frederic with him.
	Capt. & Mrs Fanshawe are settled at Clermont near Verdun where she describes herself as passing her time very pleasantly
18	Henry Jenkinson promoted to the rank of Master & Commander of the Jasper - sloop of war which is now like himself off Lisbon & he does not yet know his promotion of which his Mother is with great joy going to write him the news.
October 3	Katherine Wollaston[1] comes to Bath to drink the Waters.
9	A letter from my Brother to Charles dated August 24th - but the sad news just received from Russia did not take place till September 13th! - some papers say the 9th.
October 15	Charles has just received another letter from my Brother but the date as far back as July 19th - he sends Mrs C a present of a shawl by a Mlle du [Romerey]
	The Jasper after having been a few weeks at

---

[1] 2nd cousin - Katherine Hyde Wollaston (1764-1844) 4th daughter of Althea Hyde & Francis Wollaston.

	Portsmouth sails again.
21	A letter from my Brother to my Sister - the beginning of it dated August 24th - the conclusion September 1st - but with not quite so much news of his wife & family as in mine.
December 25	A dreadful fire in the lower town - two houses entirely destroyed & one greatly injured.

Friendship & warm affections

Without Friendship and warm affections towards connections it is impossible to be either individually happy, or to make other people so. Friendship, ready to assist, to soothe distress, or to enter with warmth into all the pleasures as well as anxieties of those we love, has always been looked on as a necessary part of an amiable character, that we are astonished when we hear of any remarkable act if friendship proceeding from a person of cold or reserved manners; but the astonishment is often unreasonable, since though coldness is seldom pleasing, it frequently forms a part of a truly excellent character... AF

1812
Events public.

	Capture of Ciudad Rodingo
February	The King supposed to be without chance of recovering the use of his senses tho' health is much as it has been for some time.
	The Prince now regent without restrictions.
April	Badajoz taken by Lord Wellington.
May 11	Mr Perceval[1], Chancellor of the Exchequer, murdered from private revenge by a man of the name of Bellingham as he was entering the House of Commons.
June 12	A new administration[2] at length selected after constant dissentions from the dismal death of Mr Perceval to the present time.
	Dreadful fire at Plymouth[3] - supposed to be not accidental.
July	Peace & friendship[4] with Russia.

Fatal shot:
the murder of Spencer Perceval
- 11th May 1812

---

[1] Spencer Perceval KC (1762-1812) remsins the only British prime minister to be assassinated - he was in post from October 1809 until assassination May 1812.
[2] Succeeding Tory Prime Minister Robert Banks Jenkinson, 2nd Earl of Liverpool, (1770-1828) - in post from 1812 to 1827.
[3] In a fire during 1812, many ropeyard buildings in the Dockyards were destroyed.
[4] 18th July - Treaty of Orebro.

August 15	News at length positively continued of which there have been reports from a great while of Lord Wellington's glorious victory in Spain - the engagements lasted from July 16th to July 23rd when after the complete defeat of the French Army, Lord Wellington on the 24th sends the account of the great yet horrid affairs from the numerous deaths on both sides - small on our side comparatively to the French, of which between 6 & 7000 remain as prisoners whilst the rest of the army fly, & whose General Merrions is wounded with the loss of arm - called the Battle of Salamanca.
	Lord Wellington created a Marquis.[1]
September	Hear of Lord Wellington entering Madrid which surrendered to him. King Joseph having flown from it some days before - he, Lord Wellington entered on the 12th of August.
October	Dissolution of Parliament.
	News of the dreadful defeat of the Russians & capture of Moscow[2] by Bonaparte - the French bulletins speak of 40,000 men killed & amongst them between 40 & 50 Russian Generals!
November & December	Wonderful success of the Russians! The French Army nearly destroyed & Bonaparte himself obliged <u>gloriously to retreat</u> before the <u>Savages</u> he designed to annihilate!
	Lord Wellington who quitted Madrid some time ago, does not proceed so successfully as before.

---

[1] 18th August - Created Marquess of Wellington in the county of Somerset.
[2] 'Battle of Borodino' took place on 14th September - reputed to have been the bloodiest single day in military history.

1813
Family events & circumstances relative to myself.

January 16	A letter from my Brother to myself, the date as far back as Nov 28 - still at Petersburgh but does not <u>appear</u> to have been employed <u>at all</u> not withstanding all we have heard! The letter however is a <u>most strange</u> one, full of the strangest & I am sure most unfounded accusations of Charles - and moreover sent me long accounts to look over, which it is impossible that <u>I</u> should understand.
23 & 25	Letters from both Mr Bridges & Mr Edwards the present managers of my Brother's affairs - fully contradicting these strange accusations,
February 26	A letter from my Brother dated 1st of January without any reference to the contents of the last, save that he is <u>ready to forgive</u>! Making a strange offer of taking one of Charles' children off his hands this Spring - to be brought up as a Page of the Empress - no explanation as to himself but expressing great his satisfaction.
March	Am informed by Katherine Wollaston[1] that what I had long suspected about Fanny Jenkinson is too true - she was [seized] at the time of her sister Elizabeth's death in the year 6 - was kept in proper care absent from her family - is called well - but alas!
April 17	Another equally or rather more strange letter from my Brother than the last! The date Petersburgh Feb. 19th.
May 6	Charles & his wife arrive after supper time.

---

[1] Katherine Hyde Wollaston (1764-1844) one of the many 2nd cousins that were the children of Revd Francis Wollaston & Althea Hyde.

10		Very severe seizure of the Gout.
20		Charles & his wife leave me.
June 6		Gout nearly departed but a violent cold brings it all back again.
August 11		Another strange letter from my Brother - this is strange as to his phrases respecting Charles - with regard to himself he continues equally mysterious & dissatisfied - this letter is dated from Moscow, June 25th - he talks of returning to Petersburgh, His sons - William is before Dantzic, George following the Emperor - but his own situation he gives not a hint.
December		After repeated inattentions and misbehaviour of Mr Spry's[1] I determined of any longer to excuse it & Doctor Parry introduced Mr Hey[2] to me as my apothecary.

Fits 28 - Attacks 120

---

[1] Several generations of the Spry family were apothacaries but AF probably referred to Joseph Hume Spry, (born 1781). In 1822 he published 'Practical Treatise on the Bath Waters' which advocated the health benefits of the waters and in 1830 he was elected Mayor of Bath.

[2] George Edmund Hay (1778-1844) apothecary in partnership as Messrs. Hay & Phinn of 3 Bladud's Buildings, Bath - it is known that this partnership from 1815 attended General d'Arblay, the husband of the writer & diarist Fanny Burney.

1813
Family marriages, deaths or births.

		Marriages	Deaths	Births
March 30	Mrs C Fanshawe a boy Henry			—
April 14	Henry Fanshawe[1]		—	
May	Lady Rivers		—	
June	Mr Henry Wollaston to Miss Buchanan[2]	—		

Economy

'…A prudent economy of fortune, or of time, by turning every part of it to use, more than doubles the value of the original quantity; whilst, on the contrary, thoughtless waste of money, or of leisure hours, costs many a sigh to the repentant spendthrift; who, years after the follies he remembers with regret, bitterly laments that which was idle lavished and is irrecoverably lost…' AF

---

[1] 4th April (baptism) - Henry Faithfull Fanshawe son of Revd Charles Fanshawe, died same year.
[2] 24th June - Henry Septimus Hyde Wollaston (1778-1867) AF's 2nd cousin - a widower married Frances Buchanan of Woodmansterne, Surrey.

1813
Marriages, deaths or Births among acquaintances or neighbours.

		Marriages	Deaths	Births
January	Mr Hodges of Boulney[1] - here in Cavandish Place		—	
	Mrs Carr[2] of the Crescent		—	
February	Mrs Andre[3] of the Circus		—	
	Old Mrs Heberden[4]		—	
April	Mrs Vane[5] of the Crescent		—	
	Sir William Scott to Marchioness of Sligo[6]	—		
	Miss Mary More[7] - sister to Miss Hannah		—	
June	Lord Vernon[8]		—	
July	Lady Charlotte Finch[1]		—	

---

[1] 5th January - Lt Col. Willam Hodges of Boulney Court, Henley on Thames.
[2] 16th January (burial) Mrs Mary Carr aged 61 years.
[3] 22nd February - Marie-Louise André (1722-1813) - daughter of Paul Girardot of Paris & mother of Major John Andre, executed by the Americans in 1780 for acting as a British spy - commemorated by a memorial in Westminster Abbey raised by King George III..
[4] 22nd February - (AF's 2nd cousin) Mary Wollaston (1730-1813), 2nd wife of Dr William Heberden the elder (1710-1801), the father of clinical observation and founder of rheumatology. The official body of British rheumatologists today is 'The Heberden Society'.
[5] 7th April - Jane Lysaght, daughter of Arthur Lysaght and Charity Wrixon and 2nd wife of Hon. Frederick Vane, son of Henry Vane, 1st Earl of Darlington.
[6] 10th April - William Scott, 1st Baron Stowell (1745-1836) Judge of the High Court of Admiralty & 2nd wife, Dowager Marchioness of Sligo, Louisa Catharine Howe.
[7] 18th April - Mary More (1738-1813) elder of the More sisters known for their work in education and philanthropy.
[8] 18th June - George Venables -Vernon, 1735-1813) - 2nd Baron Vernon of Kinderton.

[1] 11th July - Lady Charlotte Finch (1725-1813) died at St. James' Palace where from 1762 to 1793 she was the royal governess to the children of King George III and Queen Charlotte.

September	Lt George Fane[1] killed before St. Sebastian in Lord Wellington's great victory.	—	
November	Mrs Boissier[2]	—	
	Mr F Fane of Dorsetshire[3]	—	
December	Miss Fane to Major Drake[4]	—	
	Miss C Fane to Col^l Hamilton.[5]	—	

Siege of San Sebastian

---

[1] 31st August - Lt George A. S. Fane, 59th Foot, killed in the storming of San Sebastian.

[2] 22nd November - Dorothea Boissier daughter of Sir Paul Crosbie, 4th Bt & wife of John Louis Boissier (Dragoon Guards), lived at Bath until shortly before her death.

[3] 13th November - Francis Fane of Spettisbury Dorset, who died aged 61 was MP for Lyme Regis 1777-1780 and Dorcheseter 1790, 1796, 1802 & 1806.

[4] 21st December - Elizabeth Sarah Fane & Colonel Thomas Drake married at St Margaret's Church Westminster.

[5] 28th December - Charlotte Fane & John Potter Hamilton married at Walcot, Bath.

1813
Events private.

January 18	Charles has received a letter from his father - dated Oct.18th - Petersburgh
20	My Sister has heard from my Brother but the letter is to the General - date Petersburgh Dec 8th. His son George arrived at St. P with the Eagle & colours - he acknowledges a letter of mine of Sept 6th.
28	Both Charles & my Sister hear again from my Brother - Charles' letter without any date & wholly on the same business he wrote to me. My Sister's from St. P - Dec 8th but without any explanation whatsoever as to his present situation. Jenkinsons leave for the winter to Brighthelmstone.
February 23	House at Dengey very much injured by a strong wind on the night of the 18th.
	Considerable accession of the fortune of the Jenkinsons by the death of Mrs Edward Jenkinson - the house at Austen besides some income but with the condition of residence, which very much displeases. Henry Jenkinson has the good luck of gaining £90 for the reward of carrying in Dollars into Canada.
March	Charles receives a letter from my Brother of much the same date as mine of which it is almost a duplicate - making the same wild offer. W^m is returned from <u>Constantinople</u>…
	Katherine Wollaston returns to Bath.

	Mr F Wollaston[1] obtains the Living of Cold Norton in Essex.
July	Charles hears agains from my Brother who seems no longer angry nor offended by the refusal of his offer about taking a grandchild but still unexplanatory as to himself.
	Mr Jackson[2] obtains an advantageous Living in Dorsetshire.
August	A great deal of severe illness in the Jenkinson family from a sort of Scarlet Fever[3] - & poor Fanny is again ill in the way she was some years ago. They have let Austen to Genl Finch.
September	Gen¹ Finch gives up his lease by Gen¹ Jenkinson's permission at the end of a stated time & they are all in doubt again how to proceed.
December	My Sister at length hears again from my Brother but not very explicitly, Dated from the suburbs of Dantzic - Nov. 29th.
	Mr F Wollaston made Archdeacon of Essex.

---

[1] Francis John Hyde Wollaston FRS, (1762-1823) natural philosopher and Jacksonian Professor at, University of Cambridge - who on resigning his professorship in 1813 was until 1823 Rector of Cold Norton and Archdeacon of Essex - a 2nd cousin to AF.

[2] See W Jackson marriage - family section of BM&D for 1806.

[3] Disease caused by Streptococcus pyogenes, a group A streptococcal infection affecting children from the ages of 5 - 15 years with symptoms of a sore throat, fever, headache, swollen lymph nodes and a characteristic rash. Until antibiotics became available in the 20th century, scarlet fever was a serious and often fatal illness.

1813
Events public.

February	Strange letter[1] from the Princess of Wales published in the public papers.
March	All the sad enquiry ino her character in the year 1806 when she was acquitted but reprimanded for bad behaviour tho' there was no proof of positive guilt, now brought forward again & made the subject of dispute in the House of Commons & all the indecent evidence both pro & con published in newspapers!
	Death of the D'ess. of Brunswick[2].
April	Increasing Russian successes, Prussia openly joining & throwing off the French yoke.
May	Russian successes decline.
June	Armistice from the beginning of June to the 20th of July decided upon between France & the Allies.
July	News of Lord Wellington's wonderful victory[3] in Spain at Victoria - June 21.
August	Another most glorious Victory of Lord Wellington over the French, driving them nearly across the Pyrenees[4] - their commander Soult - the place St. Sebastian - the time of the action from the 30th of July to the 2nd of August.

---

[1] Published 10th February, addressed to the Prince of Wales begging access to her daughter Princess Charlotte.
[2] HRH Princess Augusta (1737-1813) elder sister of King George III, and wife of Ferdinand, Duke of Brunswick.
[3] 21st June - Battle of Vitoria when the armies of Britain, Portugal and Spain under Wellington, defeated the French army commanded by Joseph Bonaparte & Marshal Jean-Baptiste Jourdan at Vitoria in Spain.
[4] The defeat of the French under Marshal Soult during the Battle of the Pyrenees culminated into the burning and ransacking of San Sebastian. Since that time, every 31st August the City recalls the event by candlelit ceremonies.

September	Austria[1] declares war against France.
	Lord Wellington's successes in Spain continue most gloriously.
	As do those of the Allies in the North against the same enemy of the human race, as Bonaparte may be called.
November	News of the wonderful victory of the 18th of October when Leipzig[2] is taken by the Allies with the loss of nearly [every] thing of the Enemy's forces & Bonaparte himself escapes but by two hours.
	News from Spain that Pamplona[3] has fallen to Don Carlos D' Espana on the 31st of October & the garrison are prisoners of war.
	Holland throws off the yoke of Bonaparte & invites the Prince of Orange[4] to enter, who accordingly leaves England.
	Hanover restored to its ancient Government.
December	The success of the Allies & the defeat of Bonoparte proceed most wonderfully & expectations of peace are very general.
	Lord Wellington gains another splendid victory but with great loss[5].

---

[1] Austria joined the '6th Coalition' by declaring war on France in August 1813.

[2] 16th-19th October 1813 - The Battle of Leipzig fought between allied armies of Austria, Prussia, Sweden and Russia and that of Napoleon's Grande Armée of the French, Polish, Italian and Reinish Germans. This was the largest battle fought in Europe prior to World War I - involving 560,000 soldiers, 2,200 pieces of artillery and resulting in 133,000 casualties.

[3] 26th June - 31st October - Siege of Pamplona.

[4] 30th November - William Frederick, Prince of Orange landed at Scheveningen beach Holland after 18 years in exile.

[5] 10th November - Battle of Nivelle, when after San Sebastian troops of British, Portuguese and Spanish persued Marshal Soult and his army. The British 3rd Division quickly split the French army and Soult retreated further. Although the

The retreat of the French after the Battle of Leipzig

Courage
…in that of distressed circumstances, the cheerful bearing-up against adversity of a wife has often not only comforted the husband, but roused a spirit of exertion in his heart, which has perhaps extricated them both from their difficulties…
AF

British remained in the strongest position, their losses of 5,500 men were 1000 more than the French.

1814
Family events & circumstances relative to myself.

January	In consequence of a violent cold caught in December[1], am siezed by a most severe illness rendered the more disturbing by poor Dr Parry being confined to his bed since the end of last month - but by Mr Hay's care, am by about the 20th restored to nearly my usual state.
March 8	A seizure much of the same sort I had in year 11.
25	Sufficiently recovered to walk out for about half an hour.
April 30	Begin a new medicine.
May 4	A letter at last from my Brother dated like the last to my Sister from Dantzic & as far back as March 28th. Speaking of himself in the same high style as in his last; hopes soon to finish his task & then proceed to his new destination as Commander of the 6th & 28th Divisions of the Grand Army - in the Duchy of Warsaw. His son Frederic with him - the other two, one Aide de Camp to the Prince of Hoenburgh, the other to the Grand Duke Constantine[2]. The rest of the letter is filled with curiosity as to Norfolk business & anger towards Charles - both strangely addressed to <u>me</u>!
	Give Charles £3000 no ann - producing when sold out £1968 -15s.-
15	Receive a strange letter from my Brother brought

---

[1] During the winter of 1813-1814 a cold must have been inevitable for most of the population of central England - as it recorded as one of the coldest winters ever. The Thames was so frozen that an elephant was walked across the river near to Blackfriars Bridge.

[2] Konstantin Pavlovich (1779-1831) Grand Duke of Russia & 2nd son of the Emperor Paul I & Sophie Dorothea of Württemberg.

	over by his sons & tho' directed to myself evidently designed for my Sister.
29	Alteration again of medicine.
June 23	Charles, his wife, Althea, John & Ellen arrive at a little after 9 in the evening.
July 27	They all leave me at 7 in the morning.
September 13	Taken with a fit when walking in Marlborough Buildings.
18	Begin a new medicine.
October 26	Alter again.
October 29	Charles arrives about noon leaving Mrs C at Warfield.
November 11	He leaves me a little before 4 to return to Warfield.
December	Dr Parry determines on trying very frequent bleeding - hitherto without much effect…

Fits 39 - Attacks 166

St Michael the Archangel, Warfield Parish Church

1814
Family marriages, deaths or births.

		Marriages	Deaths	Births
March	Mrs Le Grys[1] of Norwich - my Brother's mother in law.		—	
	Mr Charles Fanshawe[2] of Exeter		—	
April	Mrs Payne[3] - formerly the wife of Judge Hyde		—	
	Mrs Henry Wollaston - a boy			—

Charles Fanshawe (1742-1814)
Circle of George Romney
© Valence House Museum
LDVAL21

---

[1] 15th March - Elizabeth (Bladwell) Le Grys, widow of Charles Le Grys (1726-1803) of Morton-on-the-Hill.
[2] 22nd March - Charles Fanshawe (1742-1814) Recorder of Exeter & Treasurer of the Middle Temple, died suddenly at Richardson's New Coffee House, Fleet St, London. He was the youngest son of Rr. Adl Charles Fanshawe RN.
[3] 12th April - Mary Payne, wife of Rev. John Payne of Droxford and daughter of Lord Francis Seymour first married John Hyde (1738-1796) Puisne Judge on the Supreme Court of Judicature at Fort William in Bengal. Her youngest daughter Caroline Frances Hyde was the wife of Robert Walpole (1781-1856), the classical scholar.

1814
Marriages, deaths or Births among acquaintances or neighbours.

		Marriages	Deaths	Births
January	Mrs Jubb[1]		—	
March	Mr Cobbe[2]		—	
	Lady Spencer[3]		—	
May	Miss Isabelle Fraser - daughter of the Doctor[4]		—	
	Mr Grote[5]		—	
June	Miss Cath. Burgoyne[6]		—	
October	Miss Powys[7] daughter of P Powys to Mr Simonds of Reading	—		

---

[1] 20th February - Ann Jubb died at Bath aged 86 - widow of Revd Dr. Jubb, Canon of Christ Church, Oxford.

[2] 11th March - Thomas Cobbe (1733-1814) of Newbridge, Irish politician & widower of Lady Eliza Beresford (1736-1806).

[3] 18th March - Margaret 'Georgiana' Countess Spencer (1737-1814) - wife of John Spencer, a philanthropist and one of the wealthiest men of his generation. 'Georgiana' was born at St James' Palace, where her father Stephen Poyntz was a diplomat and her mother, Anna Maria Mordaunt. a maid of honour to Caroline of Ansbach.

[4] Dr William Mackinen Fraser died earlier in September 1807.

[5] 1st June (burial) Joseph Grote (1748-1814) banker & elder son of Andrew Grote founder of Prescott Grote & Co. - merchant bankers (merged later with Nat-West Bank). He and his country residence Badgemore, near Henley on Thames, are mentioned by Mrs Philip Lybbe Powys in her letters - and consequently he was within the circle of friends enjoyed by AF's family.

[6] 4th July (burial) at Weybridge Surrey - daughter of Sir Roger & Lady Frances Burgoyne.

[7] 3rd September - Sophie Charlotte Lybbe-Powys (1796-1833) of Hardwick House, Henley - granddaughter of Mrs Philip Lybbe Powys and wife of Edward Simeon (later 2nd Bt of Grazeley).

	Miss Sibley[1] of Queens Parade	—	
November	Mrs Buchanan[2] of Marlborough Buildings	—	

Mrs Philip Lybbe Powys
1738-1817

---

[1] 31st October - Martha Sibley (1784-1814) lived at 4 Queen's Parade - she was the daughter of Revd John Sibley, Rector of Walcot.
[2] 14th December - Mrs Honoria Buchanan née Grant born 1774 - wife of James Buchanan.

1814
Events private.

January	My Sister receives a letter from Mrs Fanshawe - December 18th at Verdun[1] but soon expecting an exchange of prisoners - a draft from her husband however dated Jan 11th shows them to be still there.
February	Fanny Jenkinson is thought so much better as to be taken home again & my sister thinks her recovered.
March	Every reason to suppose that the poor prisoners are removed to Blois & are safely there after great difficulties in the journey - poor Henry Fanshawe's impendent conversation as to public affairs had occasioned him to a disagreeable removal from Clermont[2] to Verdun before they quitted that place.
	My sister received a letter from Mrs Fanshawe dated 28th February - St Gervais near Blois[3], with an account of their disagreeable removal from Verdun - that they thought themselves pleasantly enough situated where they now were but are ordered to remove again to a miserable village called [Gneret] for which place they were shortly to set forth - but have petitioned not to remove there.
April	My Sister at length again hears of my Brother in a letter to Genl Jenkinson - dated Dantzic[4] February 28th - speaking of himself very discontentedly yet with a command of 40,000 men! His sons William & George are with the Emperor & therefore now probably in Paris.
	Katherine & Emily Wollaston come to Bath to drink

---

[1] Verdun - a city in north east France.
[2] Clermont-Ferrand - a city in the Auvergne-Rhône-Alpes.
[3] Blois - on the Loire between Orléans and Tours.
[4] Gdańsk - city on Poland's north Baltic coast.

		the waters.
	15	General illumination of Bath[1].
May 3		My sister hears from Mrs H F but the date being as far back as March 10th removed to Gneret - it gives no notice of liberty or arrival in England.
May 4		Charles in London hears from Lord W^ill Fitzroy[2] who is just arrived from Calais that he had heard his brother's name mentioned as safe & at liberty but nothing further.
	7	My sister receives a letter from Anna[3] dated Paris April 30th, having met with both William & George Fanshawe - the first a colonel, second a captain in the Imperial Guards & hoping with them & her husband, very shortly to be in England.
	14	Captain & Mrs Fanshawe with George Fanshawe likewise all arrive in safety at Coombe Cottage in the evening. William to follow them very shortly when the Prince of Oldenburgh comes over.
		Henry Fanshawe after standing his trial for the loss of his ship in the year 12 is honourably acquitted at Portsmouth.
	31	William Fanshawe arrives in London & goes that evening to the Jenkinsons. He is as was expected come in the suite of the Prince of Oldenburgh.
June		Both Henry Fanshawe & Henry Jenkinson are advanced to the rank of Post Captains. Both George & William quit England again at the same time as the rest of the Russian visitors.
September		Henry Jenkinson returns to England.

---

[1] Probably celebrating the Treaty of Fontainbleau on 11th April which resulted in Napoleon being exiled on the island of Elba.

[2] Admiral Lord William FitzRoy KCB (1782-1857) son of 3rd Duke of Grafton, then a former RN officer.

[3] Anna Maria (Jenkinson) Fanshawe - wife of the captured Commander Fanshawe.

		Gen. Jenkinson sells the lease of Coombe Cottage.
October		The family of Jenkinson remove to Austen in Warwickshire.
November		My sister receives jointly with the General a letter from my Brother dated from Riga[1] - August 30th & gives notice of one at the same time received by Henry Fanshawe from my…
November		…Brother dated from Petersburgh September 24th - Frederick likewise writes - William was with them, but going to Reval[2], George gone to Warsaw. My Brother seems still in expectation of something more, yet the Emporer has given him an Arenda or Village for 12 years bringing in 10,000 roubles! On giving up at Dantzic to the Prussians, the King sent him his Order of Merit to distribute amougst his Aide de Camps so that Frederic has one.
December		My sister hears again from Russia by means of George from Warsaw & William from Reval - dates in October. W^m says he supposes she knows that his father has had an estate given him by the Emporer which brings now in 5000 roubles p^r ann! A very different story from the last.
		Charles preaches the sermon at the Charterhouse[3] meeting on the 12th & with all his family to Dengie on the 16th - after an absence ever since last Easter.

---

[1] Capital of Latvia.
[2] The former name of Tallinn, the capital of Estonia.
[3] Charles Robert Fanshawe listed as 'Preacher' for 1814 in Charterhouse records.

1814
Events public.

January	The successes of the Allies go on most wonderfully...
March	- the same
	Lord Wellington obtains a great victory over the army of Soult[1].
	English army enters Bordeaux where the white cockade[2] is immediately hoisted.
31	Allies, the Emporer of Russia & King of Prussia enter Paris, the Senate throw off the power of Bonaparte.
April	Determined on inviting the Bourbons - Bonaparte himself abdicates the throne.
	French Government declare Bonaparte to have <u>forfeited</u> the crown for himself & his place for ever & invite Louis 18th to resume his rights.
	The King of France with the remainder of the Bourbon family quit England & after the greatest attentions & respect paid to them by the Prince Regent are carried over in high state by the Duke of Clarence & land at Calais amidst the rejoicings & acclaimations of the natives[3].
	Prince of Orange[4] returns to England.

---

[1] The final campaigns of the Peninsular War when Wellesley commanded the allied army of the British, Portuguese and Spanish against forces under Marshal Soult. By crossing the Pyrenees into south-west France this lead to the capture of Toulouse and Bayonne.

[2] The symbol of the Ancien Regime as opposed to the colours of the revolutionaries.

[3] 3rd May 1814 - Louis XVIII arrived in Paris.

[4] The Prince of Orange - paying court to Charlotte, Princess of Wales.

May	News arrives of the capture of Genoa by Lord William Bentinck[1] before the news of the Liberation of France[2] had stopped proceedings
	News of the Pope's[3] entry into Rome on the 21st of last month.
	The King of France[4] 's grand entry into Paris took place on the 4th.
	Bonoparte after a journey of some danger thro' France reaches the place of his future residence with considerable income & rank as a Prince - Elba in the Mediteranean.
June	Correspondence between the Queen & the Princess of Wales published in the public newspapers relating to the first communicating to the second the desire of the Prince that she will not think of appearing at the Drawing Room[5] which the Queen intends holding on the 2nd of the month - to which the Princess agrees but revenges herself by this strange publication!
7	Arrival of the Emperor Russia & the King of Prussia into London.
20	Peace publicly proclaimed in London.
	After seeing everything worth being seen & visiting many places near London & Oxford & Blenheim

---

[1] Lt. Gen. Lord William Cavendish-Bentinck GCB GCH PC (1774-1839) Statesman & diplomat, 1st Govenor General of India who introduced many reforms including English as the official language of instruction.

[2] Napoleon defeated at the Battle of Paris on 30-31 March 1814 was forced to abdicate.

[3] Pope Pius VII.

[4] Louis XVIII.

[5] Queen Charlotte's Drawing Room presentations usually took place at Buckingham on a Thursday, so here we must assume the letter referred to was another demonstration of the continuous animousity that existed between the Prince Regent and his estranged wife.

	Castle & then going in company with the Prince Regent to the Naval Review at Portsmouth - they quitted England before the end of the month.
July 7	General Thanksgiving[1] for the Blessing of Peace all over the kingdom.
	Increase of the Princess of Wales's annuity[2] decided on by Parliament.
July 11	Strange flight of the Princess Charlotte[3] in a Hackney coach from her own home owing to anger at the Prince's displeasure to that of her Mother, from whence she is however carried back to the Prince's - but not till three in the next morning & she set forth from home in the evening of the 7th.
	Sent to reside at Cranbourne Lodge in the Forest.
	Princess of Wales goes aboard[4].
September	Great victory in America, the city of Washington[5] being taken & nearly destroyed (that is all its public buidings & stores) by a small army compared to the forces of the enemy & the command of Gen. Ross - our number 1500, that of the Americans 6000!
October	Brings news of the unfortunate defeat of our troops with Gen. Ross in America.

---

[1] Services were held throughout the nation on 7th July with a General Service of at St Paul's Cathedral where the Duke of Wellington carried the Sword of State walking alongside the Prince Regent.

[2] Increasingly unhappy with her situation, Princess Caroline with the aid of Lord Castlereagh (Foreign Secretary) finally agreed to accept an annual pension of £35,000, with the proviso that she travelled and stayed abroad.

[3] Charlotte, Princess of Wales rebelled against being sent by her father to live at Cranbourne Lodge, Windsor with all her servants replaced and no visitors except her grandmother Queen Charlotte. She ran away to her mother Princess Caroline, who eventually convinced her to return to her father.

[4] 8th August - Princess Caroline left England.

[5] 24th August - British army led by Major-General Robert Ross marched on Washington and during the night set fire to many government and military buildings, including the Presidential Mansion and the United States Capitol.

| December | Treaty[1] of Peace signed by Commissioners with America ratified here by the Prince Regent & sent for signatures in America. |

The Signing of the Treaty of Ghent
By Amedee Forestier
(Smithsonion American Art Museum)

---

[1] 24th December - Treaty of Ghent ending the War of 1812 between the United States and the United Kingdom was signed by both sides in Ghent and took effect from February 1815.

1815
Family events & circumstances relative to myself.

February 4	Walk out for about half an hour in the Crescent - the first tme since last November.
March	Dr Parry gives up bleeding & medicine for some time.
May 2	Medicines begun again.
10	Receive the heart breaking intelligence of Charles's follies!
June	More ill than for many preceeding years, having in the course of eight days twelve fits with a great deal of other illness also - Dr Parry alters medicine.
July 18	A letter from my brother dated St. Petersburgh June 9/15 - nothing clear about himself - acquainted with Charles's folly & greatly displeased.
	Stop medicine for some time.
August	Receive from my sister the most dismal account of Charles's past conduct, she tells me that his debts amount to £6000.
December	Very ill indeed.
	Medicine begun again.

Fits 58 - Attacks 115

1815
Family marriages, deaths or births.

		Marriages	Deaths	Births
February	Mrs Jackson[1] a girl.			—
April 11	Mrs C Fanshawe - a boy Robert			—
October	Mr Wollaston[2]		—	

> **Friendship and Warm Affections**
> '...Without friendship and warm affections towards connections it is impossible to be either individually happy, or to make other people so...' AF

---

[1] 14th March - Mary daughter of Louisa Hyde Jackson's and Rev'd James L Jackson of Affpuddle, Dorset.
[2] 31st October 1815 - Rev'd Francis Wollaston astronomer FRS - born 1731.

1815

Marriages, deaths or Births among acquaintances or neighbours.

		Marriages	Deaths	Births
February	Mr J Bowdler[1] the nephew of my friend Mrs H B.		—	
	Mrs Battersby - next door to me in Mrs Gambier's[2] house.		—	
March	Dr Bowen[3].		—	
April	Lady Mary Fitzgerald[4] burnt to death.		—	
	Miss Augusta Fane[5] to Capt, Keene of Swincombe, Oxfordshire.	—		
June	Dr Phillots[6].		—	

---

[1] 1st February - John Bowdler the Younger (1783-1815), essayist, poet and lawyer & brother of Thomas Bowdler who published in 1857 'The Religion of the Heart' as exemplified in the life & writings of John Bowdler.

[2] Possibly relating to the family of Admiral of the Fleet James Gambier, 1st Baron Gambier, GCB (1756-1833).

[3] 27th March - William Bowen (1761-1815) apothecary in partnership with George Spry at 1 Argyle Buildings and later 35 Gay Street. He is sometimes referred to as a physician and it is said he treated Jane Austen.

[4] Lady Mary Fitzgerald (1725-1815) was born Lady Mary Hervey, sister of the Earl of Bristol, and aunt of 2nd Earl of Liverpool - Prime Minister (1812-1827). Separated from her husband, she devoting her interest & money to Methodism being a close friend of John Wesley. She died at the age of 89, as a result of her clothes catching alight and was buried in the courtyard of Wesley's Chapel in London.

[3] 25th April - Benjamin Keene married Augusta daughter of John Fane & Lady Elizabeth Parker.

[4] 22nd July - Revd. Dr James Phillotts, Archdeacon of Bath.

	Capt. Hobhouse[1] the nephew of my friend Dr Parry, killed in the <u>great</u> Battle of Waterloo		—
September	Mrs Gwynne[2] of the Crescent.		—
October	Revd Mr Sibley[3] - Lucas Parade.		—

1815 Flag of 2nd Battalion, 69th South Lincolnshire Regiment of Foot

---

[1] Captain Benjamin Hobhouse, 2nd Battalion 69th (South Lincs) Foot - died while serving as Orderly Officer to Sir Colin Halkett commanding 5th Brigade in the 3rd Division, under the command of Major General Carl von Alten. Wounded four times during the course of the battle; late in the battle afternoon Halkett asked Wellington, 'My Lord, we are dreadfully cut up; can you not relieve us for a little while?' Wellington replied, 'Impossible!' - Halkett responded 'Very well My Lord, we'll stand until the last man falls'.

[2] 13th September (burial) Frances Gwynne (1748-1815).

[3] 22nd March - Revd. John Sibley, Rector of Walcot, Bath.

1815
Events private.

February	My Sister receives a letter from my Brother written in December from Reval but not sent till his return to Petersburgh - he speaks of this great Estate as only still in expectation! - & hopes soon to see his son Henry & Mrs Fanshawe at Petersburgh.
March	Other letters from my Brother to my Sister and to his son Henry, expressing his great displeasure towards Charles. My Sister sent him the letters to read but does not mention it to me tho' she informs me of having heard from him by means of his son George.
	The H F's are still with the Jenkinsons in Warwickshire.
18	Hear from my Sister of Henry having received another letter from my Brother - dated Jan 13th from Petersburgh empowering him to take all his English affairs into his hands & manage them for him, yet at the same time invites him <u>speedily</u> to come to him in Russia…my Brother mentions an intention of dividing Mrs Le Grys's property equally among his five sons & of doing it immediately. His own expected Estate still waits the Emporer's return.
May	Charles & all his family obliged to quit Dengie, as I hear without any chance of return - hear from him at present with Mr Faithfull.
June	Henry Fanshawe, his wife & Sophia Jenkinson pass some time in Essex - H F being now the manager of his Father's affairs & giving as far as I can judge from my Sister's letters very…uncomfortable account of Charles's management from her, also hear of Henry's having received letters from my Brother still at Petersburgh wishing for employment but as usual

	without any - the Norfolk Estate is sold for 52,000 which he thinks is too little.
July	John Jenkinson[1] has a Commission given him in the Coldstream Reg^t of Guards.
August	John Jenkinson is placed to live in London in the family of a French emigrant - the Marquis & Marquise de le [Bellinageos] a situation my Sister greatly approves on account of the French language & that he will spend his evenings singing & dancing!
	Henry Jenkinson goes on a tour which is to last for about a month in France & visit Paris.
September	Returns to the family at Alverston on the 22nd
	Charles engages in a Curacy at Kimpton near Andover, designs to take pupils.
	The Board of the Green Cloth[2] being abolished, General Jenkinson is no longer the King's Servant.
October	Death of my Mother's old servant Jane Sayers[3].
	News from my brother of William Fanshawe's being approved call up to a Regiment - the 55 Jager[4] - now as he supposes at Warsaw - invites Charles to Petersburgh.
November	Commissioner Fanshawe of Plymouth retires with a pension.
December	Hear from my Sister & from Charles himself of great difficulties as to my Brother's proposed division of his Norfolk share of Mrs Le Grys's Estate which he

---

[1] John Simon Jenkinson, enlisted as ensign in the Coldstream Guards - July 1815.
[2] AF's father Simon Fanshawe had been Comptroller of the Board of the Green Cloth (1761-1767) - named from the green baize cloth that originally cover the board's table. The Board was made up of officers of the Royal Household appointed to audit the household's accounts and make arrangements for royal travel. They also acted as a court, ruling on offences committed within the verge of the palace.
[3] 19th October (burial) - possibly Jane Sayers who died aged 75 at Old Basing, Hampshire, approx. 26 miles distant from Henley on Thames.
[4] Infantry regiment.

has not <u>yet</u> received & when he does, there are legal doubts as to his power of dividing in passing property entailed on his children at the period of his death!

Captain Robert Fanshawe RN (1740-1823)
Commissioner of Plymouth Dockyard
Circle of Joshua Reynolds
Valence House Museum LDVAL40

1815
Events public.

December	My Sister at length hears again from my Brother but not very explicitly, Dated from the suburbs of Dantzic - Nov. 29th.
	Mr F Wollaston made Archdeacon of Essex.
February	Property Tax[1] to cease in April.
March	Great riots in London in consequence of the Corn Bill proposed by Mr Vansittart[2].
	Unfortunate defeat & great loss of troops before New Orleans[3] in America in December - the news of which is now arrived.
11	Intelligence also just received of still worse news, Bonoparte having effected his escape from Elba & landed in France with about a thousand men & erected his Standard to which it is reported, that too many resort.
	Enters Lyons where he meets with no resistance.
	Treaty of Peace with America, returned from thence with signatures.
	Corn Bill[4] passed.

---

[1] During the Napoleonic wars extensive loans had been incurred by UK governments. To reduce this national debt, Prime Minister Pitt increased taxes and introduced income tax for the first time; general known as the property tax - a levy on incomes over £60. At the end of the period of war, public debate turned to the tax although the government's budget required the continuance of the income. Petitions and objections across all parties eventually prevailed.

[2] Nicholas Vansittart, 1st Baron Bexley, PC, FRS, FSA (1766-1851) was Chancellor of the Exchequer 1812-1823 - one of the longest in office in British history.

[3] 8th January - Battle of New Orleans.

[4] 23rd March (Royal Ascent) - Corn Laws were tariffs and trade restrictions on imported food, corn and other cereals into the UK. These restrictions kept prices high to favour domestic producers and traders.

	Bonoparte enters Paris on the 21st having met with no resistance whatsoever, is received with acclaimations & the poor King quits Paris - as it is reported designing to go to Lisle - but all is doubt & confusion.
April	The King of France removes to Ostend, thence to Brussels & Ghent.
	The whole South of France comes over to Bonoparte & the endeavours of the Duc D'Angouleme are completely defeated - the D'sse had some time before escaped to Spain after thence, to England. Bonoparte offers to France a form of government modelled on that of the English Constitution - the regal premier, a House of Heriditary Nobles/Lords & one of Representatives/Commons to be chosen by the people.
June	Murat[1] forced to quit his Neopolitan Kingdom which submit to the Allies - the Bay of Naples containing the Fleet surrendered to the English flag & the papal King is soon expected to return.
June	The real King of the Two Sicilies[2] again returns to Naples.
	Wonderful yet dreadful battle on the 18th of this month[3], when with horrid slaughter on all sides the French Army is <u>totally defeated</u> by the English & Prussian powers - Bonoparte flies before them to Paris where he once more <u>abdicates the throne</u> & leaves the capital.

---

[1] Napoleon's brother-in-law, Joachim Murat.
[2] Ferdinand I.
[3] Battle of Waterloo.

July	Surrender of Paris to the Allies who enter it on the 3rd - but are not yet joined by either the Russians or Prussians[1] [*Austrians*] who are shortly expected.
	Death of Mr Whithead by his own hand having cut his throat - he had for some time been suspected of insanity.
	King of France re-enters Paris on the 1st & is received with acclamations.
	Bonoparte surrenders[2] himself to the English & is brought from Rochefort where he went on board the Bellerophon, off Plymouth[3] till it is determined where he shall be permanently secured.
August	Bonoparte not having been suffered to come on shore is transferred from the Bellersphon to the Northumberland commanded by Sir G. Cockburne & sets sail on the 11th for St. Helena where he is to be kept as a Prisoner of War.
October	Joachim Murat[4] - King of Naples appointed by Bonoparte, attempts again to serve the Kingdom which he had been forced to quit on the return of the real king - is taken prisoner & put to death.

---

[1] H.C Fanshawe who used AF's diary to prepare the Dengie section of his family history 'The History of the Fanshawe family' notes that AF is in error - for 'Prussians' she should have stated' Austrians'.

[2] 15th July - from the brig *Épervier* Napoleon made his way out to the Bellerophon which had been waiting and watching under the command of Captain Frederick L Maitland. Sending a barge to receive him, Maitland brought Napoleon on board his ship where he was kept with great civility for three weeks.

[3] At first the Bellerophon lay at anchor out from Brixham but the news of Napoleon on board excited such intense local activity that Admiral Lord Keith ordered the ship to be brought to Plymouth on 26th July.

[4] 13th October - execution by firing squad.

| November | Treaty of peace[1] - signed & sent over to England between France & all the Allied Powers. |

*Scene in Plymouth Sound in August 1815
by John James Chalon.
National Maritime Museum, Greenwich*

---

[1] 20th November - Treaty of Paris.

1816
Family events & circumstances relative to myself.

January	More ill than for a long time - Dr Parry alters medicine.
March	Medicine altered again.
June	Very ill owing to a violent cold.
	Send to Frederic Fanshawe, to be remitted by his means to my Brother, the letters of Sir Richard Fanshawe[1] which he wished to see, together with my own books that he has never seen & this I have never before had an opportunity of sending to him.
July	Dr Parry alters medicine.
August 3	Taken very seriously ill & unable to leave my bedroom - fever high & in considerable danger.
10	Came down stairs.
24	Walk out for the first time in the Crescent for about half an hour.
	Dr Parry stopped all medicine for some time.
September 12	Taken with a bad fit when walking in the Crescent & carried into Mr Daubery's house[2].
	Write to my Brother by means of Henry Jenkinson who is going to Petersburgh.
October	Give Charles £50.

---

[1] Sir Richard Fanshawe (1608-1666), a loyal supporter of King Charles I and King Charles II, served as English envoy to Portugal (1661-1663) and as Ambassador to Spain (1664-1666). His many letters & despatches include those from major political figures of 17th century, as well as drafts & copies of his replies and also correspondence, written after his death, addressed to his widow Ann, Lady Fanshawe.. A considerable part of this original archive is now held in the Fanshawe Collection at Valence House Museum - but as yet, the whereabouts remains unknown of those sent by AF to General Fanshawe in Russia. It may however be that some or all of those letters are included in the archive at Valence House.
[2] Probably the home of Major Gen. Henry Daubney born c1785 resident at Royal Crescent Bath, Somerset according to probate 1853.

16 November	Begin medicine again.
	Does not agree & stop taking it by Mr Phinn's advice.
December	A letter after a very long silence from my Brother dated after the arrival of Capt. Jenkinson, yet not once naming his being come or his expectation of Charles's visit! To me his letter is full of kindness - acknowledges the letters I sent him by his son Frederic but does not mention the one carried by Henry Jenkinson.

Fits 38 - Attacks 327

Sir Richard Fanshawe 1608-1666
by William Dobson
Valence House Museum LDVAL26

1816
Family marriages, deaths or births.

		Marriages	Deaths	Births
March	Mr Fanshawe of Shabden[1]		—	
April	Mrs Bedford[2]		—	
October	Mrs C Fanshawe a girl Susannah Frances[3]			—

*John Fanshawe of Shabden 1738-1816
Courtesy of the descendants of
Adm. Dalrymple Fanshawe G.C.V.O.*

---

[1] 2nd April (burial) John Fanshawe of Shabden (1738-1816) Receiver of Fines in the Lord Chancellor's Office - eldest son of R^r Ad^l Charles Fanshawe RN.

[2] Presumably Mrs Dorothy Bedford wife of Rev'd Wiliam Bedford - their son Vice-Admiral William Bedford married Susan Fanshawe in 1808.

[3] 3rd November (baptism) Susannah Frances Faithfull daughter of Rev'd Charles & Patty Fanshawe.

1816

Marriages, deaths or Births among acquaintances or neighbours.

		Marriages	Deaths	Births
January	Mr Bathoe[1] of the Crescent		—	
February	Miss Shuttleworth[2] of James's Square knocked down & killed by a horse running over her in the street - lingered several days.		—	
March	Mrs Purvis[3] of Bennet Street.		—	
	Mrs F Bateman[4] of Lansdown Grove.		—	
April	Dr Chapman[5] of Paragon Buildings		—	
May	Mrs Glynn of Catherine Place.		—	
June	Mr Spooner[6] of the Crescent.		—	
	Mrs Elizabeth More[7] - sister to Hannah[8].		—	

---

[1] 15th January - John Bathoe (1736-1816).
[2] 10th February - Frances Anna Shuttleworth aged 37 years, died when thrown from 'her' horse in Gay St,. Bath.
[3] 25th March - Mrs Elizabeth Purvis (1752-1816).
[4] 21st March - Mrs Frances Bateman (1742-1816).
[5] 12th June - Revd. John Chapman DD. (1765-1816) Master of the Hospital of St John the Baptist & Chapel at Bath
[6] 1st June - Isaac Spooner (1736-1816) of Elmdon Hall Warwickshire - nail manufacturer and banker whose daughter Barbara married the abolitionist William Wilberforce in 1797.
[7] 14th June - Elizabeth More (1741-1816) at Wrington, Somerset.
[8] Hannah More (1745-1833) writer and philanthropist - the more famous of five More sisters who set up schools in the Bristol area and later, lived in Great Pulteney Street, Bath and also at Barley Wood, Wrington, Somerset.

July	Dr Webster[1] of Marlborough Buildings.		—
	Mrs Blundell[2] of Brock Street.		—
August	Mrs C Parry - a girl[3].		—
	Mrs Campbell of Brock Street.		—
October	Mrs Thresher of the Circus.		—
	Miss Mussenden[4] of Brock Street		—

Hannah More (1745-1816)
National Portrait Gallery

---

[1] 11th July (probate) Revd. Dr Thomas Webster.
[2] Miss Elizabeth Blundell (1756-1816).
[3] 5th August - Augusta Bertie (1816-1871) daughter of Dr Charles & Mrs Emma (Parry) Bertie.
[4] 3rd January -Caroline Mussenden (1761-1817).

1816
Events private.

	Sir Henry Rivers[1] presented by his mother to the Rectory of Walcot.
April	Receive information by letter from my Brother addressed to Genl Jenkinson (but as he says intended for us all) of the Emporer's having at last given him the long talked of Estate - the value about 4500 roubles p^r. annum, amounting to nearly £900 - a lease for twelve years but renewable at the end of that time if any of the name still continue living & in the service. My Brother is likewise named a member of the Senate & was to take the Oaths & his Seat the day after that on which he was writing & was then to go into the country on a leave of absence for two months, to visit this new acquisition.
	John Jenkinson leaves the French family to live in lodgings with a young acquaintance studying the law.
29	Am informed by my Sister of the arrival of Frederic Fanshawe in London & of his having brought the long expected papers from his father relative to the Norfolk business.
May	She tells me that Frederic Fanshawe is paying her a visit & talks of coming to see me.
	Katherine Wollaston comes to Bath to drink the waters.
	The Henry Fanshawe's at Leamington for Mrs F's health which is very indifferent & they are soon to return to Alveston.

---

[1] 22nd March 1816 to 4th June 1817 - Revd. Sir Henry Rivers, Rector of Walcot.

June	Frederic Fanshawe visits his Brother at Kimpton & then returns to the Jenkinsons at Alveston where the H Fanshawe's are likewise returned from Leamington.
	Gen[l] Jenkinson receives a letter from my Brother with a description of his Polish estate which he was returned from visiting when he wrote his letter dated May 19/31 from St Petersburgh, whither he hoped that Frederic would very soon return, as he feels very uncomfortable quite alone. He seems well pleased with his new estate which he expects considerably to improve - it consists of four villages, containing 1850 mature peasants, all bound to work for him - and of three <u>habitable</u> houses for himself (as he terms them), one of which he has decided to be in some measure furnished in case any of his family should wish to go there - but as to himself he thinks that his <u>Senatorial</u> task will chiefly confine him to Petersburgh.
July	Charles receives a letter from his Father, very much like that sent to Gen'l Jenkinson - the part relatively to Charles himself is both kind & sensible - it contains beside an invitation to Petersburgh which Charles seems to wish that he could accept of.
August	Frederic Fanshawe is sent to Paris by the Russian Ambassador[1] with a message to which he is to bring an immediate answer.
	Katherine Wollaston passes a day in Bath in her way into Warwickshire & calls on me.
	Charles makes me a visit of four days - determined to accept of his father's invitation but to go alone

---

[1] Prince Christoph Heinrich von Lieven (1774-1839) a Baltic German nobleman & Russian general - Ambassador to London (1812-1834) was also the educator of Tsesarevich Alexander Nikolaevich.

	leaving his wife & children at Mr Faithfull's. The Curacy at Kimpton is at an end as is the scheme of taking pupils. Leaves me on the last day of the month.
September	George Wollaston[1] with his three sons on a tour in France. Wm Wollaston[2] on one to Brussels & parts of Germany.
	Charles schemes all altered - has given up his intention of visiting Peterburgh till next Spring.
	Frederic Fanshawe, instead of returning to England writes from Paris that he is to set off immediately on diplomatic business for Moscow & then proceed to Petersburgh.
	Capt. Henry Jenkinson goes on a tour of pleasure to visit my Brother at Petersburgh.
	Charles after another dispute with his Rector Mr Foyle[3], settles for remaining at Kimpton till next Midsummer.
	My Sister hears from my Brother by means of Henry Fanshawe that his son George is advanced to the rank of Colonel.
October	Capt. & Mrs Fanshawe & J Jenkinson visit Charles at Kimpton. Mrs F takes little Ellen with her & they mean to pass the Winter at Brighton - changed for Weymouth.

---

[1] George Hyde Wollaston (1761-1845) - merchant banker & trader with business mainly through Genoa, Italy & England, was chairman of the Thames Tunnel Co formed by Marc & Isambard Kingdom Brunel. The tunnel was completed in 1843 and is now part of the London Underground system.

[2] Dr. William Hyde Wollaston FRS (1766-1828) brother of the above, was a chemist and physicist who is credited with the discovery of the chemical elements palladium and rhodium. He also developed a process that changed platinum ore into malleable ingots.

[3] Rev'd Edward Foyle - Rector (and patron) of Chilcombe, Dorset, and Kimpton, Hants from 1785 until his death 20th July, 1832.

	Dr Parry[1] seized by an apoplectic fit on the 25th.
November	Misses Fanshawe's of Shabden come to Bath & take a lodging for a month in Queen's Square.
December	My Sister receives a letter from Capt. Jenkinson with news of his safe arrival & pleasant reception at Petersburgh by my brother, where he finds F F returned.

Accomplishments and Taste in various Arts

'…It was said not long ago by a very sensible men…"They educate and they educate the young ladies, till they educate away their health; and they accomplish and accomplish till the accomplish loss of common understanding" And true it is, that what has very wisely been termed by Mrs H More* the 'phrenzy of accomplishment' has proved the destruction to many more essential acquirements for women than those of dancing, drawing, singing and the long etc...' AF

---

[1] Dr Parry suffered a devastating stroke which paralyzed the right side of his body and impaired his speech. He was unable to continue his medical practice and spent the remaining years of his life reading, dictating his reminiscences and supervising his farm and gardens.

1816
Events public.

March	Property Tax[1] thrown out after long disputes in the House of Commons & petitions against its continuance from almost every part of the country.
May 2	Marriage of Princess Charlotte to Prince Leopold[2] of Saxe Coburg.
July	~~Marriage of Princess Mary to the Duke of Gloucester.~~ [entry by AF in the wrong year].
July	Duke of Wellington very unexpectedly returned to England.
	Marriage of Princess Mary with the Duke of Gloucester[3].
August	Duke of Wellington leaves England again.
September	Receive from Lord Exmouth[4] an account of the complete success of the Expedition[5] against Algiers by the total defeat of the Fleet & by the submission of the Dey to all Lord Exmouth's terms - the loss on the Algerian side amounting to between 6 & 7000 men, that on the English side not more than as many hundreds - this great Victory took place on the 27th of

---

[1] In 1815, the national debt had amounted to £834 million with interest a heavy burden on taxpayers and the government retained Income (or Property) Tax temporarily, although it had been originally only a wartime emergency tax. This lead to the vote in Parliament in March 1816 when the government was defeated and the Income Tax Act was repealed.

[2] Later King Leopold I of the Belgians.

[3] 22nd July - Princess Mary, 4th daughter of King George III married her 1st cousin Prince William Frederick, Duke of Gloucester.

[4] Admiral Edward Pellew, 1st Viscount Exmouth, GCB (1757-1833).

[5] August 1816 - 'Bombardment of Algiers' - Exmouth's Anglo-Dutch Fleet attempted to end the slavery practices of the Dey of Algiers. The main aim of the expedition was successful as around 3,000 slaves were freed after the bombardment, when a treaty against enslaving Europeans was signed.

	August.
September	The Dey of Algiers submits to Lord Exmouth's terms, liberates all Christian Slaves, engages to take no more & restores the sums formerly seized by his piratical vessels & peace is finally concluded.
October	Lord Exmouth returns to England.
	Riots in many parts of the country among unemployed workmen owing to the prices of provisions.
November	Riots of the same sort in London[1].
December	Mr Hunt's endeavour to do mischief in London, having met with less success than he probably expected; made a speech in the fields near Bristol[2] the day after Xmas Day but was attended by no respectable people of any kind.
	Dule of Wellington make an English visit of a few days & returns directly to Paris.

Spa Fields Riots

---

[1] 15th November & 2nd December - The Spa Fields Riots, incidents of public disorder arising from two mass meetings at Islington which were planned by a small group of revolutionaries who invited Henry Hunt, a popular radical, to address the crowd.

[2] At a mass meeting on Boxing Day at Brandon Hill, Bristol, Hunt demanded universal suffrage - his speech fired the crowd into chanting "Hunt and Liberty" - he left Bristol nationally famous.

1817
Family events & circumstances relative to myself.

January	P Fanshawe's attempts to come but moreover before the stage xxxx fatigue suddenly but xxxxx *should (These comments un unreadable as AF has written over the original with changes..)*
	Mr Fane[1] being fortunately at Bath gives me good advice.
	[Another unreadable comment that has been written over and crossed through...] Charles whose share of my money.
24	Make a fresh Will leaving 3p^d a reduced Stock in Trustees hands for the use of Charles & his family after my death. My house & everything to Charles himself, witnessed by Mr Hay, Mr Phinn & Mr Whitaker[2].
29	Send one copy of the Will to Mr Fane - whilst the other is in my square box in the drawing room.
March	Very ill tho' not so dangerously so as in last Summer.
April	Begin a new medicine by Mr Hay's direction.
May	Very ill & more Rheumatic complaints than for a considerable time.
June 18	Give Charles £25 or rather his own rent of Dronfield.
20	Seized with a fit of the gout in my lame leg.
23	In the right leg also & very violently in both.

---

[1] AF knew several gentlemen of the Fane family but here she almost certainly refers to Mr John Fane of Worsley (1751-1824) - MP for Oxfordshire from 1796 until his death. He was the husband of Lady Elizabeth Parker, one of two daughters of the 3rd Earl of Macclesfield.

[2] Possibly Alfred Whitaker (1799-1852) then acting as Solicitor's clerk who later established a practice in the nearby town of Frome.

July 18	Out for the first time in a wheel chair & catch a very violent cold.
August 1	Out again in the same conveyance.
September	Out again sometimes in the same way yet so little able to move at all from Rheumatism & cough that walking is nearly impossible.
October	Walk a little in the beginning of the month but am soon taken very ill again with Rheumatism & a long line of dismal complaints - nine Fits in five days!
November	Charles sadly improper letters to me - much like last January's requesting total impossibilities, tho' somewhat to be accounted for from the intricacy of his affairs - make me indeed most completely wretched.
6	Give Charles £100.
December	Quite confined to the house & extremely ill owing to a most violent cold, & Rheumatism all over me but chiefly in my legs.

Fits 49 - Attacks 39.

1817
Family marriages, deaths or births.

		Marriages	Deaths	Births
April	Mr C Wollaston junior[1] to Miss Charlotte Fawcett	—		
September	Lady Rivers a daughter[2]			—
	Mrs George Wollaston[3]		—	

Truth and Plain Speaking

'...The mere affectation of truth, and of plain speaking, shews itself by a blunt manner of giving unasked, yet possibly good advice; and in a rough mode of pointing out failings, which almost always gives offence, and has often caused a lasting breach between the best friends. Advice is to be given, faults are to be reproved and there is no valuable friendship in the person whose want of courage makes him scruple to undertake the painful but truly kind office; but the manner of doing it must be attended to cautiously and tenderly...' AF

---

[1] 4th April - William Charles Wollaston (1795-1872) - AF's 2nd cousin once removed who 'married' Charlotte Jane Fawcett at Gretna Green, then five days later, from the bride's home at Leeds, they married again in her father's church.

[2] 7th May - Maria Eleanor, daugther of Sir Henry & Lady Rivers baptised at Winchester.

[3] 25th September (burial) - Mrs Mary Ann Wollaston daughter of William Luard of Witham Lodge, Essex.

1817

Marriages, deaths or Births among acquaintances or neighbours.

		Marriages	Deaths	Births
January	Duke of Marlborough[1].		—	
March	Lady Cecilia Johnston[2].		—	
	Sir John Gilman[3] of Brock Street.		—	
April	Dr Villette formerly of Brock Street.		—	
	Mrs Ramsden[4] of Brock Street.		—	
May	Rev[d.] Thomas Fane[5]		—	
	Mrs Sarah More[6]		—	
July	Mr Ravenshaw to Miss Purvis[7].	—		
August	Mr Baldwyn[8] of the Crescent.		—	
	Rev[d.] Thomas Powys[9] of Fawley.		—	
September	Mrs Blundell[1] of Brock		—	

---

[1] 29th January - George Spencer, 4th Duke of Marlborough, KG, PC, FRS (1739-1817).
[2] 3rd March (obituary) Lady Henrietta Cecilia, daughter of John West, 1st Earl De La Warr; wife of Lt.Gen James Johnston from 1762.
[3] 11th March - Sir John St Leger Gillman Bt (1756-1817).
[4] Mrs Elizabeth Ramsden died 1817 at 106 - the oldest person in England at that time was also among the richest - worth £140,000.
[5] 3rd November - Revd Thomas Fane, Rector of Adwell (1816-1817).
[6] 20th May - Sarah (Sally) More (1743-1817)- 3rd of five sisters educated to teach and also a published author - most notably 'The Good Mother's Legacy (1795).
[7] 8th July - Revd Edward Ravenshaw, Rector of West Kington Wilts married Miss Elizabeth Purvis of Darsham Suffolk.
[8] 7th August - Winthrop Baldwin of The Crescent (1724-1817).
[9] 17th August - Rev'd Thomas Powys (1768-1817) son of Philip & Caroline Lybbe Powys of Hardwick House, married Elizabeth Palgrave in 1799 - Rector of Fawley (1810-1817).

	Street.			
	Sir James Earle[2] - the surgeon who formerly married one of the Miss Potts.		—	
October	Mrs Berners[3] formerly of Hambleden.		—	
November	Mrs Powys[4] of Fairmile Henley aged 80.		—	
December	Miss Georgiana Fane to Mr Henley[5] of Waterperry, Oxfordshire.	—		
	Mrs Talbot[6] formerly Drake, sister of Lady Macclesfield.		—	

---

[1] Error by AF - see 1816.

[2] 30th September (burial) - Sir James Earle (1755-1817) surgeon-extraordinary to King George III, Master of the Royal College of Surgeons, practicing at St Batholomew's Hospital and celebrated for his speciality of removing 'stones'. His wife, Mary, was the daughter of Sir Percivall Pott, senior surgeon of 'St. Barts'.

[3] 25th November (probate) - widow of Revd Henry Berners of Hambleden, Bucks, (died 1800) former Curate at Fawley.

[4] 7th November (burial) = Caroline, Mrs. Philip Lybbe Powys (1738-1817), daughter of John Girle, surgeon of Lincoln's Inn Field, London. Her collection of diaries from the 2nd half of the 18th century provide an authentic picture of life, manners, and customs of the upper classes of the time. Extracts (published 1899) as *'Passages from the diaries of Mrs Philip Lybbe Powys of Hardwick House 1756-1808'*.

[5] 22nd November (marriage licence) - Joseph Warner Henley, PC, DL, JP (1793-1884), a Conservative polician known as J. W. Henley and his wife Georgiana, daughter of John Fane MP.

[6] 5th December (burial) - Charlotte Elizabeth Talbot, daughter of Revd Thomas Drake who lived with her husband George Talbot (1763-1836) at Temple Guiting, Gloucestershire.

1817
Events private.

January	Letters from Russia - that is from Frederic to Henry Fanshawe, make it clear that Charles & <u>his family</u> are <u>all</u> expected by my Brother.
	My Brother himself writes in the same way.
30	Charles receives a letter of the same kind from his father & Brother Frederic - inviting him <u>alone</u>.
March	Charles agrees for receiving another pupil - Lord Hay[1] the son of Lord Errol.
April	Dr Parry resigns his office as Physician to the General Hospital & on the 9th removes from his house in Bath to one on Sion Hill.
	Dr Davis[2] is elected to succeed Dr Parry.
	Letters from Russia not from my Brother, from FF & Henry Jenkinson with notice of my brother's having sold his Polish Estate for 11 years & all uncertainty as to the scheme of my Brothers coming to give the Jenkinson family the meeting in Flanders.
	Mr George Wollaston with one of his own daughters & one of his elder Brothers gone for a short time to Paris.
May	Letters again from my Brother speaking of the intended journey but without explanation or <u>when</u> or <u>where</u> the meeting is to take place.

---

[1] William George Hay, 18th Earl of Erroll, KT, GCH, PC (1801-1846), Scottish peer and politician - styled Lord Hay between 1815 and 1819, when he became heir to his father's title after his elder brother, Lord James Hay died at the Battle of Quatre Bras at Waterloo. The younger Lord Hay, educated with his older brother at Eton, must have left the school before 1814 to be placed with Charles Fanshawe for tuition and foreign travel.
[2] John Ford Davis (1773-1864), physician to Bath General Hospital 1817-1834.

June	Sir Henry Rivers[1] gives up the Rectory of Walcot to Mr Moysey[2] in exchange for Worthey.
18	Jenkinson family arrive in town preparatory to their going abroad.
28	Gen[l] & Mrs Jenkinson, five Miss Jenkinsons, Capt. J Jenkinson, Henry Fanshawe & his wife with little Ellen Fanshawe, all together sail from Dover for Ostend where they land after 8 hours & proceed for Spa[3].
July	Hear from my Sister - arrives at Spa & much pleased with her meeting with my Brother.
10	Charles sails for Ostend carrying with him his two eldest boys & two pupils - Lord Hay & Mr Johnson.
27	Hear from both my Sister & Charles of his safe arrival at Spa on the 20th - on which day they write the whole family party having just done dinner - all well & happy together.
	Charlotte & Katherine Wollaston gone for some time to the Isle of Wight[4].
August	The whole Jenkinson party leave Spain for Axe la Chapelle[5] on the 9th.
	My Brother & his set follow on the 10th - Charles removes to Brussels the week after.

---

[1] Revd.Sir Henry Rivers held several appointments as Rector simultanteously - Winchester St Swithun (1813-1829), Walcot (1816-1817), Martyr Worthy (1817-1829) & Winchester St Peter Cheshill (1818-1818).

[2] Revd Charles Abel Moysey (1778-1859) - Rector of Walcot from 1817, appointed Archdeacon of Bath in 1820.

[3] The town in Belgium famed for mineral springs.

[4] Steamship ferries first began to operate from Portsmouth to Ryde in 1817 but were quickly withdrawn so we must assume the Wollaston sisters travelled across on one of the two daily return trips offered by the Ryde Wherries, introduced in 1811. Originally the difficulties getting ashore at Ryde might have deterred two ladies, but fortunately Ryde Pier was built in 1814 and resolved the problems.

[5] Aachen - on the border between France and Germany.

September	Charles returns to England on the 9th meets Mrs C at her father's at Warfield from whence he goes to Norwich & finds their long delayed business there going on better than for some time.
	Mr Freeman[1] of Fawley offers Charles the Living of Fawley, vacant by the death of Mr Thos Powys and by resigning the Living of Dengey he finds himself able to accept.
	Hear from both Jenkinsons & my Brother now at Ghent & happy to hear of the payments already made in Norfolk with expectation of the whole being soon concluded - as also greatly pleased with Fawley hopes…
	Kath Wollaston at Mr Jackson's[2] in Dorestshire.
	Mr G Wollaston & his daughter return England owing to the death of his wife[3].

George Hyde Wollaston
(1765-1841)

---

[1] Mr Freeman, descendent and heir of William Freeman who rebuilt Fawley Court, Henley-on-Thames during the 17th century. The Living of Fawley became vacant following the deaths of Philip Lybbe Powys (1809) and his son Thomas Powys (1817).

[2] Revd W Jackson - the husband of Louisa, a sister of Katherine Wollaston.

[3] Family connections of his wife Mary Ann Luard had led to George Hyde Wollaston of Clapham Common becoming a merchant and banker in Genoa importing and exporting between England and Italy. After the death of his wife he quickly liquidated his business and returned to England. His position was probably eased by having recently inherited the estate of his uncle, General West Hyde.

October	Mr & Mrs Freeman[1] spend three weeks at Bath & show me the greatest attention extremely wishing for Charles's soon coming to settle at Fawley.
	Hear from my Sister that they have taken a house for a month at Ghent but seems very doubtful whether they shall stay or go.
November	My Brother designs if he can, to remain at Ghent till his affairs in England are setted, but believes that business in Poland must call him there before the beginning of next year - speaks with much displeasure of Charles & of Norfolk dilatoriness.
16	Charles preaches his first sermon in Fawley church after having gone tho' all proper forms of his institution on the Thursday before.
December	He & all his family invited to take up their residence at Fawley Court till his own house at Fawley is ready to receive him - which he hopes will be early in the course of next year.

Fawley Court 1811

---

[1] Owner of Fawley Court - Strickland Freeman and his wife.

1817
Events public.

January	Mr Hunt attempts speeches at Bath which are as little attended by respectable people as they were at Bristol.
8	The Prince Regent insulted by the mob - stones thrown & bullets it is thought, fired against the State Carriage, the glasses of which were broken as he was coming from the House of Lords where he had opened the present session of Parliament.
February	A secret committee[1] appointed for the purpose of discovering many & dreadful conspiracies for the distruction of all laws, governmnt & indeed religion - very much in the former French style!
March	Habeas Corpus Act for a time suspended[2] till after the people now confined on the suspicion of High Treason can be brought to their trial.
June	Very serious & alarming riots[3] in Yorkshire, Derbyshire & Nottinghamshire put a stop to sooner than could have been expected.
June	Watson[4] & some more of the state prisoners strangely

---

[1] February 1817 - Extract from Hansard - Commons Sitting: *'Report of the Secret Committee of the House of Commons, respecting certain meetings and dangerous combinations'*.

[2] 4th March (Royal Assent) - 'An Act to empower His Majesty to secure and detain such Persons as His Majesty shall suspect are conspiring against His Person and Government.'

[3] 9th & 10th June - 'The Pentrich Rising' began near Pentrich in Derbyshire when Jeremiah Brandreth led nearly three hundred working men armed with pikes, scythes and a few guns to march on Nottingham. Part of their revolutionary agenda was to wipe out the National Debt but they were infiltrated by a government spy and the riot was quickly quashed. Brandreth and two other leaders were executed at Derby.

[4] Watson was tried first in a week long trial where the main prosecution witness was a man called Castle who had been on the organising committee of the meetings. However, when Hunt, was called as a defence witness he accused Castle

	acquitted of positive treason[1] on their trial!
September	The Prince Regent goes out on a sailing party[2] & is four days at sea - very much delighted with his tour.
	Fine weather[3] & consequent fine crops produce a most plentiful harvest.
	Lord Amhurst unsuccessful embassy to China which set forth in Feb 1816 - returned to England after the loss of their vessel the Alceste which struck on a rock near a desert island in the month of February of this year but by means of an East India ship procured from Batavia, after considerable difficulties & distress, the whole crew arrived home in safety in <u>August</u> - tho' entered here after September. A relation J B Martin[4] was on board the Alceste, a midshipman.
October	Rioters at Derby brought to trial when four are condemned to death, many to transportation & some pardoned.
November	Queen, Princess Elizabeth & Duke of Clarence come

---

of conspiring to make others commit treason and with the defence lawyer, he exposed Castle as a person who entrapped others. Although not directly called a spy, he was cited as 'an agent provocateur'. The jury accepted that defence and found Watson not guilty. Consequently all cases against others were dropped.

[1] 15th November & 2nd December - 'The Spa Fields Riots' relating to public disorder at two mass meetings at Spa Fields in Islington.

[2] The Prince Regent, an enthusiastic leisure sailor was the first of the royal family to join the Yacht Club at Cowes and 'Royal' was added to the club's title in 1817.

[3] 'Good' weather was probably the subject of conversation during 1817 as the previous year has been called 'the year without a summer'. Temperatures in Europe were the coldest recorded between 1766 to 2000 and major food shortages had resulted.

[4] AF has confused her relative's initials, she mean to refer to the early naval voyages of Admiral Sir William Fanshawe Martin, 4th Bt, GCB (1801-1895) who was the eldest son of Admiral of the Fleet Sir Thomas Martin & Catherine, a daughter of Captain Robert Fanshawe RN, Commisioner of the Royal Dockyard at Plymouth.

4	to Bath which is illuminated on the night of their arrival, to the houses in Sidney Place[1] which the Queen has engaged for a month, designing to drink the waters for this time.
6	Death of the Princess Charlotte[2] after being delivered two hours before, of a dead male child.
8	Queen to leave Bath for Windsor.
	Three of the condemned prisoners at Derby are put to death for treasonable proceedings - whilst the fourth, Weightman is respited till the 14th.
19	Magnificant funeral of the Princess at Windsor[3], the day kept throughout the Kingdom with prayer & signs of grief carried to an excess of absurdity & not in propriety. An indecent riot took place in St. Paul's Cathedral owing to the immense crowds who visited the church more in the stile of attendants on a theatre than in a place of worship, crying out for the Service & Anthem to begin, breaking windows & behaving with impious witness.
24	Queen returns to Bath - to leave it again Dec. 23rd.

---

[1] 'At half-past four they entered the city, full an hour before they were expected. The royal carriages, escorted by the 15th Dragoons, passed Walcot Church and proceeded by York House, down Milsom Street and through New Bond Street to Sydney Place...a brilliant illumination took place in the evening, the streets were crowded to excess, and not the least riot or confusion occurred'. *The Annuals of Bath*.

[2] The tragic death of Princess Charlotte Augusta of Wales (1796-1817), only child of George, Prince of Wales (later King George IV) and heir to the British throne. Her widower was Prince Leopold of Saxe-Coburg-Saalfeld.

[3] 'The Prince Regent was so grief stricken he was unable to attend his daughter's funeral at St. George's Chapel, Windsor where she was interred alongside her baby son. The sudden loss of the popular Princess impacted the entire nation - places of public entertainment closed out of respect, and on the day of her funeral the streets of Windsor were lined with mourners.' *The Royal Collection Trust*.

| December | Mr Hone[1] a printer tried for publishing a profane libel & parody of the Church Liturgy - pronounced <u>not guilty</u> by a strange quibble of words; tho' <u>proved</u> guilty of printing the parody, yet that it was with no <u>intention</u> to blaspheme! |

*Princess Charlotte of Wales
(1696-1817)
by George Dawe
Museum of New Zealand*

---

[1] 18th, 19th & 20th December - Trial of William Hone (1780-1842) writer, satirist and bookseller often regarded today as one of the fathers of modern media. His three court battles against government censorship took place at the Guildhall before special juries and his victory began the fight back for press freedom in Britain.

1818
Family events & circumstances relative to myself.

January	Receive most mortifying letters from both my Brother & my Sister as to Charles offering improper schemes of various kinds. Wants to sell the Living of Dengie! - to which my Brother[1] refuses his consent.
March	Mr Wilkinson brings me a small payment from the tenant Bunting (£10) who promises more before May Day. Mr W thinks he shall be in Derbyshire soon after that time when he will see & speak to Bunting & manage my business for the remainder of the year.
April 14	Out once after five months confinement, very ill again immediately from attacks & violent increase of both cough & Rheumatism.
30	Receive heartbreaking accounts from Charles of his situation & give him £250 which tho' it distresses me - cannot really serve him!
July	Great increase of all my complaint - scarcely able to walk at all, but go out now & then in wheel chair with more pain than comfort - violent cramp in my sides & chest of more consequence than when the limbs only were affected.
August	Charles makes me a visit of four days, speaks in the highest terms of the good refs of the Freemans to him & of the good done by them in their parish, expresses himself as most comfortably fixed at

---

[1] Gen. Henry Fanshawe's refusal to sell and the outrage expressed by his sister's 'exclamation mark' in her journal is not surprising. The Patronage of the Living or Advowson of the Parish of Dengie had been held by succeeding members of their family since 1561/2 when the Manor was purchased by Henry Fanshawe, Queen Elizabeth's 1st Remembrancer of the Exchaquer.

	Fawley.
	A letter from my Brother at Petersburgh
November	Hear again from my brother at Petersburgh wondering at my silence - yet I write constantly.
	Extremely ill for more that three weeks owing to violent cold increasing all my old complaints.
December 2	Send Charles £32 paid by Bunting to Mr Wilkinson with a promise of more before the end of the year.
	Taken <u>very</u> ill on Christmas Day

Fits 50 - Attacks 86.

Attention

'...True attention is full as often to be found in the lower, as in the higher classes of life: and the attentions of a servant who remembers, and takes care to move a chair or shut a door, because he knows his master likes it; the present of a particular sort of flower from a cottager, after an absence perhaps of years; - these sort of natural attentions, which are certainly not the produce of education, are truly pleasing; whilst those of over-strained civility are to apt to be affected and not proceeding direct from the heart, to sink into

1818
Family marriages, deaths or births.

		Marriages	Deaths	Births
September	Charlotte Jenkinson[1] on the 21st at Lyons.		—	
November	Ellen Faithfull Fanshawe[2].		—	
December 19	Mrs C Fanshawe a girl Emily.			—
	Anna Maria Fanshawe[3]		—	
	Frances Christiana[4] a daughter of Dr & the late Mrs Haggits		—	

---

[1] Charlotte Frances Jenkinson seventeen year old daughter of AF's sister Frances Jenkinson and Gen. John Jenkinson born March 1801.

[2] 1st November - Ellen Faithfull Fanshawe (1811-1818) - *'Little Ellen'* daughter of AF's nephew Charles who was travelling with the Jenkinson family (see May 1817 Events Private).

[3] Anna Maria Fanshawe (1787-1818) elder daughter of AF's sister and the wife of Henry, eldest son of Gen. Henry Fanshawe (Russian Service).

[4] 18th December (burial) - Frances Christiana Haggitt (1806-1818) grand-daughter of Capt Robert Fanshawe ('The Commissioner') and daughter of Prebentary of Durham, Revd Dr & Mrs Christiana Haggitt.

1818
Marriages, deaths or Births among acquaintances or neighbours.

		Marriages	Deaths	Births
January	Mrs Leman[1] of the Crescent		—	
March	Mrs Wilmot[2] formerly Miss Parry in childbirth of twins who live.		—	
	Mr Jaffray[3]		—	
August	Mr Emerys[4] of St. James Square		—	
	Lady Colebroke[5].		—	
December	Dr Murray[6] who was seized much about the same place as Dr Parry in the year '16, with an apolpletic fit.		—	
	Lady Araminta Monck[7] of Queens Park Buildings		—	

---

[1] 21st January (burial) - Mrs Frances Leman (1743-1818), heir of her father, the barrister William Nynd and wife of Thomas Leman. Her first husband was Brigadier Gen. Alexander Champion of East India Co, Commander in Chief, India.

[2] 22nd March - Emma Eardley-Wilmot (Dr Parry's daughter) died after twins born 12th March: Augustus Hillier Eardley-Wilmot (died 1892) & Selina Mathilda Caroline Eardley-Wilmot (died 1902).

[3] 28th March - Alexander Jaffray died at Cheltenham aged 83.

[4] 2nd August - Possible James Emery (1762-1818) buried at Wedmore, Somerset.

[5] 26th August - Mary Colebrooke (née Gaynor), lived at 31 Marlborough Buildings Bath. Wife of Sir George Colebrooke 2nd Bt. MP - a merchant banker who became bankrupt in the financial crisis of 1772. After a period abroad and after recovering some of his fortune, he settled in Bath and became well known as a philanthropist.

[6] Dr John A Murray.

[7] 26th December (burial) - Lady Araminta Monck (1729-1818) née Beresford. daughter 1st Earl of Tyrone wife of George Paul Monck, MP.

1818
Events private.

January	Charles & all his family settled in the Parsonage House[1], Fawley.
February	He goes to London for a few days on business to Mr Fane's.
March	My Brother leaves Ghent on his return to Peterburgh - his son William with him.
April 'falsely by Day's fraud'	[*The entry made has been heavily struck through to obliterate - the only word discernible is the first - being Charles*].
May 1	Receive a letter from my Sister who with all her family, & the Henry Fanshawe's are at Lille, intending for Paris - & wondering at Charles's silence.
	My Brother at Warsaw.
	The whole Jenkinson family, H Fanshawe & his wife with little Ellen - all at Paris.
June	Katherine Wollaston passes two days in Bath in her way to Mr Churchill's in Gloucestershire & brings Miss A Day back to her parents.
July	Mr G Wollaston with his two sons passes thro' Bath & calls upon me.
	The Jenkinson family after passing some time at Paris remove for a months to St. Germains en Laye[2] for Mrs Fanshawe's health from whence my Sister now writes designing very shortly to remove on their long projected…

---

[1] 'Fawley, one I suppose of the most elegant parsonages in England, commanding from a very good house a prospect uncommonly noble' Extract *'Passages from the diaries of Mrs Philip Lybbe Powys, Of Hardwick House (1756-1808).*
[2] Small historic town about 12 miles east of Paris.

July	…tour thro' Switzerland to the South of France for the winter - which is the present plan. Henry Fanshawe is, she says, gone to England for a short time on the Norfolk business & she hears my Brother at Petersburgh in a letter dated May 30. Her own is of the 14th of this month.
	William Fanshawe has another new Regiment of Carabiniers.
	Two of the Wollastons, Harriet[1] & Anna[2] are most providentially preserved from any material injury from a bad overturn of an open carriage in which they were driving near Cheltenham & out of which they both were thrown. It fell on the manservant & the horse was killed by falling into a pit.
August	The hurt which at first appeared trifling proves very serious - Anna Wollaston's <u>hurt</u> of her leg being discovered to be a fracture & Harriet's bruises preventing a return home as late as this middle of …
September	Receive a dismal letter from my Sister who with her whole immense party are stopped in Lyons in their way to the South of France - every day expecting the death of Mrs H Fanshawe or Charlotte Jenkinson. Henry Fanshawe had joined them again before their quiting the neighbourhood of Paris.
29	Another letter from my Sister still at Lyons with notice of Charlotte's release on the 21st. Mrs H F still very ill & as soon as the funeral is over, their intention is to proceed on their southern journey.
November	Anna Wollaston still obliged to use crutches in consequence of her hurt - Harriet's pains in her head still considerable yet good hopes are given of

---

[1] Possibly Henrietta Hyde Wollaston 1768 - died Chislehurst 1840.
[2] Anna Hyde Wollaston - born London 1769 - died Greenwich 1830.

	recovery by their medical attendants.
	Little Ellen Fanshawe dies at Marseilles on the 1st of the month - of a violent bilious fever & my Sister writes a dismal account of the event as likewise of her own sad situation, every hour expecting the death of Mrs H F with whom however she means if possible to set forth the day following the date of her letter (Nov 2nd) for Hyeres[1] where they design to pass the winter.
December	Hear from my Sister of the General's having taken a house for six months certain at Hyeres where Mrs H F still continues in the same uncertain yet dangerous state as has so long been her fate. Both Fanny & Harriet Jenkinson very ill & my poor Sister in dreadful spirits - their son John had just joined them having on the return of the Coldstream to England, obtained a leave of absence for six months.
29	Hear from my Sister of the release of poor Mrs H F on the 13th - they design to remain at Hyeres till towards Spring.

---

[1] Hyeres, the oldest of the resorts on the French Riviera, was extremely popular in the 18th & 19th centuries with British and later Americans, where for reasons of health, many famous personalities, writers and artists 'wintered'.

1818
Events public.

January	Attempt at Paris to assassinate[1] the Duke of Wellington by firing at him - happily without effect but the culprit is not yet discovered.
	Repeal of the Act passed last year for a temporary suspension of the Habias Corpus Act.
April	Attempt to assassinate Lord Palmerston by firing at him without serious effect tho' there was a slight wound. The assassin's name is Davis[2] - taken & assigns no particular cause for the fact which he does not pretend to deny.
	Marriage of Princess Elisabeth[3] to the Prince of Hesse Homberg.
May	Marriage of the Duke of Cambridge[4] to Princess Augusta of Hesse.
June	The Queen very ill & in considerable danger.
10	Parliament dissolved by the Prince Regent in State.

---

[1] 11th February - Marie André Nicolas Cantillon (1781-1869) attempted to assassinate the Duke of Wellington when he was in Paris as the commander of the allied occupation after the defeat of France. The would-be assassin's shot missed and he was captured by the Parisian police. When brought to trial, he was acquitted when his lawyer told the jury that as the ball from his pistol could not be found at the scene, his conviction would stain the honour of the nation. Cantillon received a bequest of 10,000 francs in the will of Napoleon I.

[2] 8th April - Palmerston as Secretary of War (1809-1828) had considerable success but as he attempted to remove many of the abuses in his department, animosity built up. As a result, Lt. Davis attempted to assassinate him on the War Office steps but his shot caused only a slight hip wound. When Davis was brought to trial, Palmerston, with characteristic magnamity paid for his defence counsel.

[3] 7th April - Daughter of George III - Princess Eiizabeth (1770-1840) married Frederick, Landgrave of Hesse Homburg.

[4] 7th May, in Kassel & also 1st June at Buckingham Palace - son of George III, HRH Prince Adolphus (1774-1850) married Augusta of Hesse-Cassel (1797-1880).

July	Duke of Kent[1] marries the Duchess of Lieningen.
	Duke of Clarence[2] marries the Princess Adelaide of Mieningen
	Prince & Princess of Hesse Homberg[3] leave England.
	Duke & Duchess of Clarence[4] on the sea on a tour of some months.
	The Duke of Gloucester[5] alone sets forth to visit Italy but leaves his Duchess to take care of the Queen.
August	New Parliament chosen & prorogued till November.
October	Great meeting[6] of the Sovereign Emperors of Austria & Russia, the King of Prussia & the Ministers of the other Potentates of Europe at Aix[e] la Chapelle when the withdrawing of the armies of occupation from France is decided upon.

Duchess of Kent 1818
by George Dawe
Royal Collection of Belgium

---

[1] 11th July (at a double wedding with his brother Edward, Duke of Kent) - William Duke of Clarence (1765-1837) son of George III and later King William IV, married Adelaide of Saxe Mein (1792-1849).

[2] 11th July (at a double wedding with his brother Edward, Duke of Kent) - William Duke of Clarence (1765-1837) son of George III and later King William IV, married Adelaide of Saxe Mein (1792-1849).

[3] Prior to leaving England the newly married couple honeymooned in Brighton staying at the home of her elder brother The Prince Regent.

[4] The Royal couple travelled to Hanover where during their stay lost their hoped-for first child. Greatly distressed, they travelled further into Europe for a while.

[5] William, Duke of Gloucester (1770-1834), son of George III's brother, Prince William of Gloucester. His wife was his cousin Princess Mary (1776-1857), daughter of George III - married 22nd July 1816.

[6] 1st October - the opening of the Congress of Aix-la-Chapelle.

November	Death of the Queen[1] after long & dismal sufferings took place on the 17th.
December 2	Magnificent funeral at Windsor whither the Queen's body is removed from Kew where she died - the Prince Regent attends & throughout his mother's illness showed the most affectionate attention.
	The King's unhappy condition worse[2] - that is more lost than ever. Great difficulties & delays in proving the Queen's Will[3].

*King George IV as Prince Regent
by Henry Bone 1816
after Thomas Lawrence*

---

[1] 17th November, Queen Charlotte died at the age of 74 at Dutch House (Kew Palace) in the presence of the Prince Regent, her eldest son.

[2] Although George III lived until 29th January 1820, it is doubtful he was ever able to be told of his wife's death.

[3] The Queen's will was written the day before she died. Her estate of £140,000 comprised mainly of her jewels and caused problems for many years. On her death the jewels were claimed by the Prince Regent, who passed them to his heir William IV. When Queen Victoria came to the throne; as Queen Charlotte's granddaughter she believed the jewels were Crown property and would be passed to her but Prince Ernest, Victoria's eldest surviving uncle and the head of the House of Hanover disputed ownership. He considered they were Hanoverian property and an agreement was not reached in 1858 when the jewels were delivered into the hands of the Hanoverian Ambassador.

1819
Family events & circumstances relative to myself.

January	Still very ill, a blister[1] applied on the 8th.
February	Send Charles £20 received in post of payment from Bunting of Fanshawe Gate.
March	All old complaints greatly increased & a violent cold & pain in my face makes eating a sadly difficult operation.
20	Notice of being to pay a very considerable sum (£147) as my share in the Allotment of Land which is to produce considerable increase in the value of Fanshawe Gate.
	Bunting sends another payment of £30 remitted to me by Mr Croft & tells me of a desirable tenant instead of Bunting at a very advanced rent - Bunting still promised payment of the remaing £29-8s still due.
	Mr Wilkinson gives me notice of the same good news & I answer both letters by accepting of Mr Lowe as my Tenant & enquiring as to the expense of the allotment.
April 2	After confinement since last October, walk out for half an hour in the Crescent.
15	Send Bunting's £30 to Charles & tell him my good Derbyshire news.
24	Pay to Mes[srs] Crompton & Co the £147.9.6 about which I heard in March.
June	Am paid by means of Mr Croft; Bunting's last payment of which after all deductions £25 is remitted to me.
15	Hear from Mr Murray that I am entitled to £54

---

[1] Blistering involved placing hot plasters onto the skin to raise blisters that would be then drained to purge the system of various conditions.

	stock in the 3 p^r c^t com ann. - due to me on my 18 shares at £3 p^r share in the West Jersey Society[1].
July	Extremely ill.
August	A very serious hurt by a scald of my left arm which took place during a fit.
September	Charles makes me a visit of six days & leaves Bath on the 4th of this month - goes on very comfortably at Fawley & takes four pupils.
October	Mr Wilkinson in Bath for about a fortnight & tells me that the Lease will certainly be sent to me for signature together with the half years rent which Mr Lowe owes me from Lady Day[2] last (when I accepted him as my Tenant) with the deduction however of my share of the expenses for the drawing of this long delayed lease & of my gift to Mr Croft.
	Very seriously ill from a violent cold begun last month & reducing me to really uncommon weakness with total loss of appetite & power of swallowing any solid food.
November	Continue very ill tho' appetite mends.
December	Receive a letter from Mr Croft with an account from Mr Lowe of his having paid for me £58.6.5 for fencing & walling the new land instead of the half years rent due to me a Michaelmas[3]! No news of the lease which ought to have come to me before this time & was to have been made out at £97 the first year - & £110 afterwards.

Fits 35 - Attacks 125.

---

[1] West Jersey Society, held valuable lands in New Jersey and Pennsylvania and made stock available to smaller investors.

[2] 25th March.

[3] 29th September.

1819
Family marriages, deaths or births.

		Marriages	Deaths	Births
March	Miss Wollaston[1] (daughter of the Archdeacon) to the Rev^d J W Trevor	—		
October	Althea Wollaston[2] (daughter of the Archdeaon) to the Rev^d H R Moody	—		
December	Miss Haggitt[3] to the Rev^d J Baker	—		

Rev'd Henry Riddell Moody
(1792-1873)

---

[1] 31st March - Frances Althea daughter of Revd. Francis Wollaston Archdeacon of Essex to Revd. John William Trevor, Rector of Llanbeulan, Anglesey.
[2] 29th October - Althea, daughter of Revd. Francis Wollaston Archdeacon of Essex to Revd. Henry Riddell Moody - Rector of Charsham.
[3] 14th December - Catherine, daughter of Revd Francis Haggitt & Christiana Fanshawe to Revd. James Baker later Rector of Nuneham Courtney, Oxon.

1819

Marriages, deaths or Births among acquaintances or neighbours.

		Marriages	Deaths	Births
January	Mr Leman[1] of the Crescent to Mrs Hodges of St. James Square.	—		
February	Mrs Hamilton[2] of the Crescent.		—	
March	Mrs Western[3] of Brock Street.		—	
April	Mrs Saunders of the Circus.		—	
	Mrs G Calvert[4] of Queen's Parade.		—	
	Mrs Fitzgerald[5] of St. James Square.		—	
	Lady O'Bryan[6], her mother of the same place.		—	
	Mrs Anne Calvert[7] of the Circus		—	
	Lady Burton.[8]		—	

---

[1] 14th January - Revd Thomas Leman to Mrs Frances Hodges.
[2] 29th January - Mrs Betty Hamilton.
[3] Mrs Jane (Calvert) Western (1736-1819) widow of Thomas Western of Gt.Abingdon died 1781.
[4] 15th April - Mary (Haddock) Calvert (1749-1819), wife of George Calvert.
[5] 19th April (burial) - Catherine Fitzgerald (1780-1819) of 17 St James Sq., Walcot, Bath.
[6] 24th April - Lady Ann Nichola (Nancy) (French) O'Brien (1747-1819) widow of Rt. Hon. Sir Lucius O'Brien, 3rd Bt Leamaneh, MP, Clerk of the Crown & Hanaper in Ireland.
[7] Wife of Lt. Gen. Sir Harry Calvert, KGC - Colonel of the 14th Regiment of Foot & Adjutant-General of the Forces.
[8] 27th April - Dame Barbara Burton (1746-1819) widow of Sir Robert Burton MP.

June	Rev\^{d\} Mr Andrewes[1] to Miss Heberden, daughter of Dr. Heberden	—		
July	Mrs Roquemont[2]	—		
	Mrs Duke[3] - both sisters of Mr Freeman	—		
September	Mr Erdley Wilmot[4] to Miss Chester	—		
	Mrs Martha More[5] (sister of Hannah)	—		
	Dr Percival[6] of Marlborough Buildings	—		

---

[1] 10th June - Thomas Gerrard Andrewes to Elizabeth C Heberden - her mother was a Wollaston cousin of AF.

[2] 7th July (Burial) - Charlotte de Behague Roquement (c1761-1819) of Appleshaw, Southampton - a sister of Strickland Freeman of Fawley Court married in 1798, Francis Joseph Henry, Chevalier De Behague Roquemont.

[3] 9th July - Emily Duke (1760-1819) wife of George Duke, married 6th February 1798 at Quarley Hampshire.

[4] 31st August - Sir John Eardley-Wilmot (1783-1847), later Lt. Gov. of Van Deiman's Island - widower of Emma Parry, daughter of AF's doctor married his 2nd wife Elizabeth Chester (d.1869).

[5] 14th September - Martha 'Patty' More (1747-1819) - younger of the five More sisters who were writers and early advocates for female education.

[6] 23rd September - Dr Edward Percival - published 'Practical observations on the treatment, pathology and prevention of typhus fever' (printed by Richard Cruttwell of Bath 1819).

1819
Events Private.

February	My Sister accounts of her family greatly improved - in point of spirits much improved with their situation at Hyeres & with John Jenkinson having joined their party - they now think of extending their tour into Italy & not returning home before September.
	Charles receives another pupil, a son of Lord Archibald Hamilton[1] & agrees with Mrs Harper[2] (formerly Heathcote) to take her only son on lower terms - £150, being much younger than his other youths.
March	Receive a letter from my Sister still at Hyeres (dated on the 17th) intending to set out on the following day for Nice from where she will give me a direction where to direct, but is uncertain whither they shall proceed - they part with H Fanshawe at Hyeres who intends for England & in the winter to go to his Father at Petersbugh.
April	Hear again from my Sister at Nice, intending however in a few days to set out for Genoa. Hear again from Genoa - all uncertain where they shall proceed next.
May	H Fanshawe returns to England & Charles meets him in London - & afterwards makes a visit to Fawley Parsonage - much to Charles's satisfaction.

---

[1] Lord Archibald Hamilton (1770-1827) - although he never married there were rumours of a child from an affair with his cousin Lady Augusta Murray the unrecognised wife of the Duke of Sussex, son of George III.
[2] Elizabeth (Heathcote) (1767-1852) & Revd. George Harper DD. Rector of Stepney.

	The Morton[1] business is settled at last & the shares of the five Fanshawe brothers will be £3,418* a piece.
June	Charlotte & Katherine Wollaston[2] take a house for a few months at Eltham in Kent & hope finally to fix there.
August	After an Italian Tour fixing nowhere for many weeks & passing a short time at Geneva, my Sister writes news of the General's having taken a house for two weeks longer at Vevay[3] in Switzerland after which they may determine where to fix for the winter.
	The three Miss Fanshawes[4] set forth on a fashionable visit for a few weeks in Paris.
	The apothecary, Mr Hay is seized with the same urge for travelling & sets forth for Paris.
	After another visit to Fawley, H Fanshawe sets out for Petersburgh & carries his cousin Capt. Randall[5] with him.

*Note recorded in the original diary by H C Fanshawe - relating to the total sum of 'the Morton business'
$3418 \times 5 = 17090$

---

[1] The probate regarding the Le Grys estate in Norfolk.
[2] Revd. Francis Wollaston, Rector of Chislehurst died in 1815 when his single daughters would have needed to vacate his rectory. Their new home three miles distant at Eltham presumably suited the sisters, for Charlotte who died in 1836 was still resident. Her sister Katherine died in 1844 and both were interred in the Wollaston vault at St Nicholas Church, Chislehurst.
[3] Lake Geneva, Switzerland.
[4] Daughters of John Fanshawe of Shabden - Penelope, Catherine Maria & Elizabeth.
[5] Capt. Randall, the son of Judith Le Grys & Benjamin Randall - a first cousin of the younger Henry Fanshawe.

September	Mr Francis Faithful[1], brother to Mrs C F is presented to the valuable living of Hatfield by the Marquis of Salisbury to whose son[2] he has been tutor - it is said to be worth £2,300 p^r annum.
October	The Jenkinsons determine on passing this approaching winter at Vevay or Lausanne - is still uncertain. H Jenkinson was set off for Italy when my Sister wrote on the 20th Oct.
	Charles is appointed Chaplain[3] to the Duke of Clarence.
November	C & K Wollaston purchase the house at Eltham which they have for some time liked.
December	Miss Fanshawes - that is eldest & Elizabeth Jane returned from their foreign tour - but Catherine extends it to Italy[4] where she designs to pass the winter.
	A letter from my Brother dated Oct.31/Nov.12 - speaks of his great pleasure in seeing four of his sons together at Petersburgh - Henry however not in good health, William a Col of a Reg^t of

---

[1] Revd. Francis Faithfull (1786-1864) Canon at Lincoln & Rector of Hatfield - a strict disciplinarian with a boarding school at the rectory, a 'prep' school for aristocratic boys prior to entering public school.

[2] James Brownlow William Gascoyne Cecil (1791-1868) - politician usually known as Lord Cranbourne whose son Robert Gascoyne-Cecil, 3rd Marquess of Salisbury was three times Prime Minister. This family were related to the Fanshawe family through the marriage in 1745 of Thomas Fanshawe of Parsloes and Mary Gascoyne, daughter of Sir Crisp Gascoyne.

[3] HRH Prince William, Duke of Clarence, later King William IV.

[4] The sketch book completed on this journey by Catherine Maria Fanshawe is now among the Archives of Valence House Museum. It contains many drawings and water colours of peasants and others she encountered on the journey. Elizabeth Fanshawe, also a talented artist, painted many scenic views of the landscape they saw in Northern Italy. In the 21st century her work has been studied by academic research geographers who track changes in Italy's alpine landscape. A copy of their resultant publication is also available at Valence House Museum.

	Carabiniers, George with the rank of Col still belonging to the Archduke Constantine's establishment & Frederic just appointed Gentilhomme-de-la-Chastre to the Imperial Court.
27	Hear again after a long silence from my Sister, her letter dated on the 15th of this month from Lausanne where they have taken a house by the month & hitherto seem to like it. John has left them to join his Reg^t in England which by purchase he is advanced - from Henry they have heard at Florence.

Print - The Peterloo Massacre published by Richard Carlile
(Manchester Libraries)

1819
Events public.

March	Great disputes about the reduction of the King's Establishment & appoint of the Duke of York[1] to the care of his person with or without salary.
April	Duchess of Cambridge lays in of a son[2].
May	Duchess of Kent the same, of a daughter Victoria[3].
July & August	Great disturbances amongst the lower kind of people calling themselves Reformers & Lovers of Liberty, Riots & misbehaviour at Manchester[4] encouraged by too many who ought to know better & fermented to a violent degree by the the long mischevious <u>Hunt</u>, are really alarming.
September	The same kind of riots in parts of Scotland.

---

[1] Prince Frederick, Duke of York, entrusted with the care of his father George III during 1819.

[2] 26th March - Prince George, Duke of Cambridge (1819-1904) grandson of King George III and cousin of Queen Victoria.

[3] 24th May - birth of Queen Victoria - died 22nd January 1901.

[4] 16th August - this event came to be called 'The Peterloo Massacre, taking place at St Peter's Field, Manchester. It resulted in the death of 18 people with another 400 - 700 injured after cavalry charged a crowd of approximately 60,000 demanding reform of parliamentary representation. The Napoloenic Wars had resulted in great unemployment and the situation was aggravated by unusual weather conditions causing poor crop production. At a time when only 10 percent of men had the vote, and petitions from the industrial north for reforms were all rejected by Parliament, by 1819 the 'Radicals' began to mobilise ordinary men into protest. Manchester's Industrial growth resulted in the forming of unions and their inspired speakers such as Henry Hunt were a target for arrest. Consequently, when this meeting started the local yeomanry were ready to charge through the crowd then after a woman and child were killed, the crowds protested - then, they too were brutally cut down.

October	Terrible meetings all over the Kingdom breathing the most rebellious & blasphemous sentiments into the minds of the ignorant who are taught to admire the men who pride themselves in being Deists & in ridiculing Christianity - & who styling their cause Radical Reform are to make the poor equal to the rich & to new model the government of the country! Hunt however & Carlile[1] the printer of impious publications, seem to lose ground amongst these wise reformer - but much mischief & rebellious principle is afloat.
November	Carlile condemned to pay a very heavy fine & to three years imprisonment[2].

Truth & Plain Speaking

...Plain speaking is a most commendable quality in all ranks of people, and it all our transactions we must wish to be connected with those whose truth and plainness leave us no doubts as to confiding in their honesty... AF

---

[1] Carlile had quickly become an important figure in radical circles, and was due to speak on the hustings at St Peter's Field alongside Henry Hunt on 16th August 1819. Unlike Hunt, he avoided arrest so was able to published his eye-witness account of events of that day in Sherwin's Weekly Political Register on the 21st August with the headline 'Horrid Massacre at Manchester'. The next issue, was the Register's last but then six days later, Carlile published the first issue of The Republican which continued until December 1826.

[2] Carlile was tried in October 1819 being charged with blasphemy and seditious libel for his work on the Republican and also for publishing the works of Paine. Found guilty, his sentence was six years in Dorchester Gaol but he still continued to write in The Republican published by his wife Jane with the help of Davison. It was Carlile's claim that sales of The Republican reached 15,000 a week during his trial. *Edited extract from Manchester University Press - June 2018.*

November	Parliament having met much earlier than is usual at this time of the year with a view to taking some measures that may check the present disturbances. Ministry appear as they ought to lead & the oppositionists to be really a trifling <u>Minority</u>… Hunt & his <u>Radical</u> set are it is to be hoped in earnest despised by both parties.
December	Parliament adjourns till February in next year after carrying many most reasonable & proper bills for the future preservation of peace & prevention of the numerous blasphemous publications which have of late produced so much mischief.

Richard Carlile, publisher. (1790-1843)

1820
Family events & circumstances relative to myself.

January	Begin the year with great illness
February	Strange & mortifying letters from Charles full of improper schemes for raising money he at present wants & wishing me to join by sending papers of my own as security for the £2000 he wants to borrow which I am forced to refuse - the title deeds of <u>my</u> house - as security for <u>him</u>!
March 12	Receive the Lease letting Fanshawe Gate to (* 14) John Lowe at £110 p^r. ann - for me to sign which owing to a mistake by terming me A F widow, cannot be done without alteration?
23	Correct the mistake myself by the direction of M^{essrs} Paitson & Charge[1] of Chesterfield & return the lease to them - signed by me & witnessed by Mr George Edmond Hay & Mr William John Church.
March * 14	A letter from Mr Murray gives notice of having paid Mr Drummonds £936 as on *[my actions of works I asked them to carry]*.
January * 9	Messrs Drummond sends me the transfer receipt of £54 Stock paid to me in the 3 p^r c^t consolidated annuity according to Mr Murray's[2] letter as likewise of his having paid £5-17-9 dividend due to me in October last in West New Jersey Society.
April 14	Another letter from Mr Murray with notice of £9-3-6 to be paid to me.

---

[1] Attornies in practice at Chesterfield.
[2] A notice by Alexander Murray of Symond's Chambers, Chancery Lane London - Treasurer of West New Jersey Society, regarding a forthcoming General Court of Proprietors 25th March at 1pm. *New Times (London) 11th March 1820.*

	Walk out for the first time for about half an hour in the Crescent since last September.
May	Extremely ill for nearly three weeks with increased old complaints & several <u>fresh visitors</u> - Rheumatism, Gout being the leaders.
	Receive a letter from Mr Croft with an account from Mr Lowe of the expense he has been at in walling in the new land. In the drawing of the lease with numberless activities which I know nothing about & maybe right or wrong, but which with the assistance of a gift from me to Mr Croft of £10 - makes out the sum of £110 for which the Estate was let, was due to me at Lady Day last - & is now verified to me by means of this strange letter in the form of an account with a surplus balance of three shillings & 9d !
June 24	Gout in both legs - Rheumatism not giving way & all other complaints as bad as ever.
July	Once more in wheel chair but considerably worse with faintings & many additional complaints owing to extreme weakness till towards the end of the month, when I mended a little.
	Gave Charles £50.
August 14	Charles makes me a visit of five days.
September	Extremely ill with Rheumatism & great increase of fits, with a violent cough & bowel complaints.
October	Equally ill.
	Receive letter from Mr Croft containing £55 being Mr Lowe's rent for the half year due at Michaelmas.
November	Illness greatly increased.

December	Very alarming faintings, my new complaints being determined to proceed from a collection of Black Bile[1] which for a long time resisted all medicine - reduced me to extreme weakness & certainly occasioned considerable danger. On the 11th Mr Wollaston, being accidentally present during a very terrible seizure administered the Sacrament - on the 26th began to mend a little - continue very weak & ill on to the end of the year.

Fits 33 - Attacks 103

---

[1] Black bile is a sign of a possible life-threatening problem. Black or brown vomit indicates possible internal bleeding from the stomach - relative to a gastric ulcer, gastritis or inflammation of the stomach lining from other causes.

1820
Family marriages, deaths or births.

		Marriages	Deaths	Births
May	Mrs Trevor - a girl[1]			—
	Frederic Fanshawe to a French woman named Frances[2] Chini	—		
November 29	Mrs C Fanshawe a girl - Maria[3]			—
~~May~~	~~Mrs Moody a girl - died September~~			—

---

[1] 20th April (baptism) - Frances Elizabeth, daughter of Frances Althea & John William Trevor.
[2] Francoise Marie Sumain de Château-neuf - name Francisca is given for the mother at the birth of son Constantine Fanshawe in Russia during 1830.
[3] Maria Faithfull Fanshawe (1820-1906) - married Arthur M Hoare on 13th October 1853. Mrs Hoare eventually became the keeper of this diary before passing it to her niece. See the letter to HC.

1820
Marriages, deaths or Births among acquaintances or neighbours.

		Marriages	Deaths	Births
January	Mrs Holroyd[1].		—	
February	Mr Keeling[2] - for years an invalid.		—	
March	Benjamin West[3] - the famous painter		—	
May	Archdeacon Thomas[4] of Bath		—	
June	Lord Gwydir[5] - suddenly at Brighton of gout in the stomach.		—	
July	Mrs Charles Eyre of Gay Street		—	

---

[1] 22nd January (burial) - Sarah M Holroyd (1739-1820) died in Bath: sister of John Baker Holroyd, Earl of Sheffield.

[2] 3rd March - James Keeling (1762-1820).

[3] 11th March - Benjamin West, (1738-1820) - an American artist who achieved success before arriving in Europe, by painting famous historical scenes. After settling in London and gaining the patronage of George III by helping to launch the Royal Academy, he followed Sir Joshua Reynolds as president and was appointed Surveyor of the King's Pictures. West is known to have visited Bath where among others he painted in 1812, a portrait of John Eardley Wilmot, a son-in-law of Dr C Parry.

AF was obviously an early admirer of West's work for in 1792 whilst still living at Shiplake, she replicated his resurrection painting in tapestry. HCF in the HFF states that this tapestry was presented and installed in the chapel of Trinity College, Oxford but recent enquiries made to the Chapel Historian could not confirm the information.

[4] 22nd May - Josiah Thomas (1760-1820) Archdeacon of Bath from 1817 until his death.

[5] 29th June - Sir Peter Burrell, 1st Baron Gwydyr PC (1754-1820) a politician who through his wife's inheritance held the appointment of Deputy Great Chamberlain of England. He is also noted as an early cricket enthusiast who in 1787 was involved in the foundation of Marylebone Cricket Club.

		Dr Moysey[1] (Archdeacon) to Miss Stewart.	—		
September		Mr Augustus Pechell[2]		—	

John Eardley Wilmot - 1812
by Benjamin West (1738-1820)
Yale Center for British Art, Paul Mellon Collection

---

[1] 24th June - Charles Abel Moysey married Elizabeth Susanna Stewart.
[2] 19th September - Augustus Pechell of Berkhamstead Hall - Receiver General of HM Customs died aged 67. His widow Sarah (1762-1839) was co-heir of her father Revd Thomas Drake DD, Rector of Amersham, with her sister, the wife of a near neighbour, Thomas Dorrien.

1820
Events private.

January	John Jenkinson in England.
March	The Jenkinsons still in Lausanne & all indecision about letting their house at Alveston. My Sister's letter full of messages which I am to deliver to Charles about Lucerne seeds[1] & to Mrs Hopton about her not having yet been paid the money she expected.
	Katherine Wollaston reaches Mr Trevor's house at Carnarvon where she means to remain till her neice is safely brought to bed.
April	Mrs Hopton is paid & I am desired by her to give notice of it.
May	My Sister's letters give notice of the same uncertainty as ever about quitting Lausanne yet hints at a return to England in the Autumn, perhaps passing next Winter at Brighton, perhaps in the Continent - but all seeming to depend chiefly on the letting of Alveston. She also hints at Frederic Fanshawe's shameful marriage with a woman he has long kept as his mistress - her account all very bad & very mysterious.
	Henry Fanshawe arrives to London with an intention of applying for a ship.

Medicago Sativa

---

[1] Lucerne Seeds - Feuille de Luzerne (Medicago Sativa), commonly called Alfalfa - a highly nutritious herb containing vitamins, calcium, potassium, phosphorus and iron used in the prevention or treatment of various illnesses.

May	Mr Panchen[1] seized with a paralytic stroke the day before the arrival of Emily & Anne Wollaston[2] to Hunt[3] again where they find Mrs Panchen in the greatest anxiety her husband having lost the use of one side & being in considerable danger.
June	Henry Fanshawe visits his brother at Fawley & *[this whole section has been written over - possibly it relates to the illness of Charles' wife and her distressing situation and is perhaps too private to be looked into more]*.
	Dr Moysey of Walcot Parish is appointed Archdeacon of Bath.
July 1	After silence since last December, hear again from my Brother - his letter dated May 24 & June 26 - & not even naming his son Frederic's marriage & yet saying he believes he's at Paris.
	Henry Fanshawe makes another visit at Fawley.
August	Mr Hay again seized with the French travelling disorder.
November	Mr & Mrs Charles Wollaston come to Bath; lodge on the South Parade & he comes to me very frequently - am too ill as yet to become acquainted with her.[4]
October	Hear from my Sister at Strasburgh, at length set out on the journey to England, but all uncertainty as to when it will positively take place, or where they shall live when it does happen - & the whole month is filled with continual uncertainty & contradiction as

---

[1] Revd W Panchen (1774-1828) Vicar of Huntingdon, St Mary and St Benedict (1803-1828), married in 1803 to AF's 2nd cousin, Mary Hyde Wollaston (1760-1843), eldest daughter of Francis Wollaston & Althea Hyde of Chislehurst, Kent.
[2] 'Amelia' Hyde Wollaston & Anna Hyde Wollaston - unmarried younger sisters of Mrs Panchen.
[3] Huntingdon.
[4] *[this entry is repeated in the continuation of the year's private events - presumably AF wrote it first on this page in error]*

	to future plans, together with sad & reasonable sorrow as to poor Fanny's [1]melancholy state of mind, making it impossible for the peace of the rest of the family that she should continue to live in her Father's house. My Sister agrees to final separation, F J & she travel to England with some friends of the name of Dale (or Day) & is to board with another friend at Norwich.
November 11	Quite unexpectedly, as the beginning of the letter speaks of a chance of them passing the winter abroad it ends with the news of the Jenkinson family being landed at Dover on te 9th & going for the present to Brighton.
November	Mr & Mrs Charles Wollaston[2] come to Bath, lodge on the South Parade & he comes to me very frequently - am too ill as yet to become acquainted with her.
December 2	The final separation between Fanny Jenkinson has now taken place, she is gone to live with a Mrs Lohr[3] at Norwich paying £100 pr ann for board & lodging which my Sister thinks too much. They are at present well pleased with their situation at Brighton.
	Charles goes to Town to marry his late pupil Lord Erroll[4] to one of the Miss Fitzclarence[5] (daughter of the Duke of Clarence) - the ceremony is performed

---

[1] Fanny Jenkinson's medical condition is not clarified here, but the family's concerns were for her mental health - see biographical notes for AF for further information.

[2] Rev'd Charles Hyde Wollaston (1772-1850) Vicar of East Dereham, Norfolk & his wife Sarah Willett (Ottley) - married 1795.

[3] Possibly relating to the family of William Lewis von Lohr and Mrs Harvey Eliza Lohr residing at Norwich during this time.

[4] 4th December 1820 - marriage of William George Hay, 18th Earl of Erroll, KT, GCH, PC (1801-1846), styled Lord Hay from 1815 to 1819.

[5] Lady Elizabeth FitzClarence, one of the ten illegitimate children of King William IV and the Anglo-Irish actress Dorothea Jordan (1761-1816).

	with great magnificence. Charles is received in the most gratious manner by both the Duke & Duchess & spends his three days in London at St. James's.
17	After only a fortnight passed at Mrs Lohr's, Fanny changes her mind - finds she cannot be happy unless she lives at home & without waiting for her Mother's approval of the change in her schemes, returns suddenly to Brighton & they are now to live all together again. They have already changed their house & taken another at Brighton where both H Fanshawe & John Jenkinson have joined the party.
	Dreadful fire in the lower part of Bath, totally consuming Assembly Rooms[1] & endangering Upham's Public Library - happily no lives lost.

Comforts of Bath: The Ball, 1798
by Thomas Rowlandson.

---

[1] Bath's Lower Assembly Rooms, were built in 1708 for Thomas Harrison and overlooked Parade Gardens between North Parade & Bath Abbey. A ballroom was added in 1720 which was then enlarged during 1749 and also in 1810. Known as 'The Kingston Assembly Rooms' they were destroyed by fire in December 1820 but after rebuilding, they survived until demolition in 1933.

1820
Events public.

January	Death of the Duke of Kent[1].
	Death of the poor good old King[2] at the great age of 81 & ½ - on the 29th of this month.
31	The present King George 4 proclaimed immediately in London.
February	The King extremely ill in considerable danger but symptoms called favourable by the 4th, mends considerably & by 10th out of danger.
	Dreadful murder of the Duke de Berri[3] as he was coming out of the Opera at Paris.
25	A dreadful plan[4] for the murder of many of the prime ministers during a grand dinner at Lord Harrowby's is happily discovered & prevented on the exact day it was to have been executed. A great number, not less than 16 of the conspirators are already secured & it is hoped that more will still be found out - they all appear of the very lowest order of beings - but much mischief seems unhappily afloat.
29	Dissolution of Parliament & the calling of another announced.

---

[1] 23rd January - Duke of Kent died of pneumonia - his only daughter, Princess Victoria (later Queen) less than a year old.
[2] 29th January at Windsor Castle.
[3] 14th February - Charles Ferdinand d'Artois, Duke of Berry, younger son of King Charles X of France was assassinated at the Paris Opera by Louis Pierre Louvel a Bonapartist.
[4] Known as the Cato Street Conspiracy - a plot to murder all the British cabinet ministers and Lord Liverpool, the Prime Minister. The conspirators planned the assassination to take place when all the cabinet were at dinner together.

March		Terrible altercations going on in Spain[1] under the pretence of liberty & virtue - sadly resembling the former horrors of France & the King <u>accepts & refuses</u> the laws of the Constitution to which he is slave to - thereby which he some time as reigned with perhaps too unrestrained a power.
March		Great disturbance of the Radical sort both in the north of England & in Scotland.
April		Meeting of the new Parliament & the King for the first time, goes to the House & makes the opening speech in form - on the 27th of the month.
		Five of the leaders in the conspiracy for the murder of the ministers assembled at Lord Harrowby's are condemned[2] for High Treason & executed accordingly - five more to transportation.
May		Hunt & several more very noted <u>Radicals</u> are found guilty of Treason & sentenced[3] to imprisonment & fines accordingly. Hunt's term to be two years & half close confinement & bound to keep the peace for five years after - may it be kept! Several more of the same description of Radicals are found guilty & condemned to transportation for life.
June 5		The Queen in defiance of all prudence & propriety is wild enough to return to England (6th) - & takes up her abode at the house of Alderman Wood[4] in South Audley Street, London.

---

[1] Ferdinand VII re-established absolutist monarchy in Spain, rejecting the liberal constitution of 1812 but the revolt in 1820 led by Rafael del Riego forced the restoration of the constitution and began three years of liberal rule.
[2] 28th April - trial sentencing.
[3] 15th May - trial sentencing.
[4] Matthew Wood (1768-1843), of 77 South Audley Street and Little Strawberry Hill: *'He enticed Caroline, with assurances of popular acclaim, which he had orchestrated in advance, to disregard their advice and return to England with him. They arrived in London on 6 June, with Wood, whose 'vulgarity' shocked the establishment, sitting beside the queen*

June	On the same day a message from the King is delivered both in the House of Lords & the Commons by Lord Liverpool & Castlereagh - of his intention immediately to proceed to legal enquiries into the Queen's conduct.
	After many unsuccessful attempts to conciliate angry spirits, the Queen's conduct is to be examined by a secret committee & on their report further proceedings to be decided.
30	The mob admire Queen Caroline!
July	The Queen continues courting the people & meets with too much admiration from the rabble to whom she shows herself every day at windows to smile & be cheered with shouts & hussas! Addresses are brought from various parts of the country & answered by her Majesty, directed towards the King & his Ministers.
	Parliament adjourns till August when the trial is to take place.
	A dreadful insurrection of the people takes place in the Kingdom of Naples[1] where the King submits & accepts of the Constitution which (as in Spain) is forced upon him!
September	After a long & most indecent examination of witnesses against the Queen, the Parliament adjourns till the 3rd of October, to give her party time to prepare their reply to the accusations which

in an open carriage and acknowledging the cheers of the crowds lining the route. Satirized as 'Mother Wood', a notorious brothel-keeper and procuress, but also lauded as the 'Foe to Oppression', he accommodated her in his house in South Audley Street for two months before she moved to Brandenburgh House, Hammersmith'. Extract: The History of Parliament:- the House of Commons 1820-1832.

[1] The revolution in Naples, against King Ferdinand I of the Two Sicilies who was forced to make concessions and promise a constitutional monarchy. As a result of this success the Carbonari in the north of Italy also began to revolt.

	appear too true to admit of denial with any degree of reason.
	A violent revolution originating among the military takes place in Portugal[1].
October	The Queen proceeds in impudent courting of the lower order of people who are always charmed by such conduct into calling black white. Parliament carries enquiries which tho' bringing evidence of the very act of adultery, sufficiently prove the licentious character of the woman whom the mob admire.
November	The Queen very sufficiently proved to be totally unworthy of her situation, yet further proceedings are deferred till January in the next year to the 23rd, of which month the Parliament is prorogued - which the mob term the <u>Triumph of Innocence</u> & occasion a forced illumination not only in London but indeed all over the Kingdom.
	Scandalous addresses in compliment to her Majesty & expressing the most rebellious sentiments towards the King & the Constitution are presented from too many otherwise respectable parts of the country & are answered by the Queen in, if possible, as scandalous manner.
29th	The Queen returns public thanks at St Pauls, for her deliverance from her accusers, attended by a sort of mock procession of the very lowest & the people who hussa & continue to admire!

---

[1] The 'Liberal Revolution' began with a military insurrection in the north of Portugal at Oporto and quickly spread through the country. As a consequence, the Portuguese Court, exiled in Brazil since the Peninsular War returned in 1821.

December	Duchess of Clarence lays in before her time of a daughter, christened Elizabeth![1]
	Loyal Address presented from all ministers to the King and the Queen seems to lose ground in the minds of even her mob friends - if any newspaper stories are to be believed.

'Reflection (To be, or not to be?).'
Cartoon by George Cruickshank 1820

---

[1] 10th December - Elizabeth Georgiana Adelaide - the baby's death occurred within three months - on 4th March 1821.

1821
Family events & circumstances relative to myself.

January	Charles makes me a visit of five days.
	Gave Charles £25 - his own rent!!
	Toward the end of the month nearly as ill as in December last.
February	Still worse.
March	After confinement since last September - go out in a wheel chair but am far from better after the attempt.
April	Out only in a chair - walking being quite out of my power - from very increased illness.
	A letter from my Brother gives notice of his intending to overlook his son Frederic's improper marriage & of the approaching one which he seems to like of William with a German lady of the name of Meisser[1].
June	Very ill indeed with various complaints till towards the middle of June when I was out
July	sometimes in a wheel chair - & on the 18th of July was seized with Gout in both legs more violent than I can before have had.
28	My Sister & her youngest daughter, Harriet Jenkinson make me a visit.
August 6	My Sister & Harriet leave me for Cheltenham where Sophia drinks the waters under Dr. Boisragon's care.
20	Charles & his eldest son Charles make me a five days visit.
September	Jenkinsons return to Alveston

---

[1] Pauline de Meisner (1791 - died 9th Dec.1856).

	In the end of the month am taken most violently ill with a complaint in the stomach & bowels which is at present very general in Bath.
October	Occasionally troubled with slighter attacks of the same kind of disorder.
November	With the addition of Rheumatism in all my limbs & a most violent cough to all my long list of complaints I am very ill indeed one time eight fits in the course of four days.
December	Conclude the year with distressing increased illness.

Fits 45 - Attacks 56

1821
Family marriages, deaths or births.

		Marriages	Deaths	Births
March	Mrs Hopton		—	
May	Miss Jane Wollaston[1] - daughter of the Archdeacon.		—	
	Mrs Moody a girl[2] who dies in September		—	—
September	Mr William Wollaston[3] son of George Wollaston		—	
December	William Fanshawe to Mlle Meisser[4]	—		

---

[1] 5th May (burial) - Jane Wollaston aged 17 at St. Peters Church, South Weald Essex - her parents were Archdeacon Francis Hyde Wollaston and Frances Hayles.
[2] 13th May - Amelia Moody daughter of Revd. Henry & Maria (Wollaston) Moody
[3] 24th September - William Luard Wollaston (1799-1821) died at Ryde I.O.W having matriculated from St, John's Cambridge in the autumn of 1820.
[4] Pauline de Meisner (1791-1856) daughter of Johannis de Meisner.

1821

Marriages, deaths or Births among acquaintances or neighbours.

		Marriages	Deaths	Births
January	Mr Boissier[1] formerly of Bath.		—	
	Mr Oliver[2] of the Crescent.		—	
February	Lady Dunalley[3] of the Crescent		—	
	Mrs Bowen[4] wife of D^r B of Margaret[5] Chapel.		—	
March	General Donkin[6] - 94 years of age.		—	
May	Mrs Piozzi[1] for some years		—	

[1] 2nd January - John Louis Boissier (c1742-1821) died at Cheltenham. The son of a French Protestant exile, and the husband of Dorothea Howard Crosbie (1757-1813) - married at Bath July 1788.

[2] 16th February (probate) - Richard Oliver (1761-1821) lived at 25 The Crescent from 1815. Son of Isabella & Thomas Oliver of Leyton, Essex, he was an Antigua merchant and member of the East India Co. His wife Maria, was a daughter of Nathaniel Brassey, the banker. In 1791 his portrait was painted by the celebrated Georgian artist, George Romney.

[3] 26th February - Catherine, Lady Dunalley, daughter of Francis Sadlier and Catherine Wall. Her second husband Henry Prittie (1743-1801) was created 1st Baron Dunalley of Kilboy in 1800.

[4] 24th May - Mrs Elizabeth Bowen wife of Rev'd Dr John Bowen.

[5] St Margaret's Chapel (c1773) at Brock Street was designed by John Wood the Younger being based on Hadrian's Arch in Athens and entering via the arch, the chapel hidden behind houses was reached - the church was destroyed during WW2.

[6] 6th March - General Robert Donkin (1727-1821) died at Bristol. He was born in Morpeth, Northumberland and served in the army for nearly 80 years being promoted to the rank of General in 1809 - *"General Donkin passed a long life of the most unsullied honour and with the greatest respectability, without sickness and apparently without uneasiness of any sort and although he has served in a great verity of climates and had been engaged in nine actions and in seven sieges, he was never absent from his duty either from illness or wounds'* (extract: obituary in The Gentleman's Magazine 1822).

	an inhabitant of Bath - Gay Street		
	Mrs Freeman[2] of Fawley Court.	—	
October	Mrs Phinn[3] wife of Mr Phinn the partner of Mr Hay.	—	
December	Mr Freeman[4] of Fawley Court at Meisieres in France where the death took place November 26th	—	

Hester Thrale Piozzi
1786
National Library
of Wales

---

[1] 2nd May - Hester Thrale died aged 81 at Bristol although in her later years she was resident at 8 Gay Street, Bath. From a Welsh landowning family, she was married first to Henry Thrale, a wealthy brewer, and after to Gabriel Mario Piozzi, a music teacher. Highly intelligent, Hester Thrale is distinguished as an author, diarist and patron of the arts. She was a close friend of Samual Johnson and her legacy of personal independence is reflected through her view of 18th century life, to leave her undoubtedly a very early feminist.

[2] 12th May (burial) - Mrs Elizabeth (Strickland) Freeman (1751-1821).

[3] 21st October (Burial) - Mrs Caroline Dorothea (Bignell) Phinn (1788-1821) of Princes Buildings married December 1811.

[4] Strickland Freeman, owner of Fawley Court and the Living at Fawley - husband and 1st cousin of Elizabeth Freeman. The couple who died only 6 months apart, left no direct heir to their extensive estate.

1821
Events private.

February	The Wollastons leave Bath very much to my grief, his attention during my illness having been great indeed.
March	Mrs Hopton who seems by all I have heard of her to be one of the oddest of all odd characters, appearing to be in bad circumstances yet hoarding up sums of money in flower pots, bas(o)ns & sewed up in her clothes - £1200 having been found in that manner in her house; has left to Charles by her Will £100 (this is 50 to him & 50 to his wife) & £1000 to Mrs Jenkinson independent of the Gen[1] - the remainder of her property, including her house in Rivers [Hurst], to Mrs Morris who was her cousin by having married Mr Morris, the cousin of Mrs Hopton's father. Mr Morris has a legacy of £200 - but his wife alone all the rest. Mrs Hopton was the daughter of my father's sister Elisabeth[1], & the widow of three husbands - Albert, Hale & Hopton.
	Death in a sadly sudden manner of poor William Browne's wife, owing to a sore throat not taken proper care of by the apothecary who pronounced her out of danger just before her death - a mortification having taken place. Charles had the melancholy task of burying her & had not for years before entered Shiplake Church!
May	Jenkinsons leave Brighton & return to Alveston - find their place greatly injured by the carelessness of their tenants during their absence & are very much dissatisfied - but mean to let it again if they can.

---

[1] 'Mrs Hopton' was AF's 1st cousin - the daughter of her aunt Elizabeth Fanshawe (born 1714/5) and her husband Corbyn Morris (Commissioner, writer & economist).

	Charles much dissatisfied by poor Mrs Freeman's death in the absence of her husband whose unkindness can only be incurred on the scene of madness!
June	Alveston more in favour with the Jenkinsons - my Sister fancies poor Fanny quite well & is charmed with her <u>inconceivable efforts</u> to serve the poor by whom <u>she is adored!!!</u>
July	Charles meets with a dreadful accident by the overturn of a gig; himself, his wife & little Emily thrown out of it, he is dragged along on the ground. Mrs C most severely bruised but fortunately none of them as it is said seriously hurt - that is no bones broken!
28	My Sister & Harriet Jenkinson come to me at Bath - full of incomprehensible schemes as to Alveston, the present thought seems to be living there in the Summer & if they can let their house, at some public place in the Winter.
August 6	Leave me for Cheltenham where Sophie Jenkinson is to meet them - remain there for more than a month & then return to Alveston
September	- as uncertain as ever where to pass the ensuing Winter.
25	A letter from my Brother - date August 18/30 - gives notice of William Fanshawe's being advanced to the rank of Major General and keeping his Reg^t besides.
November	The General lets the house at Alveston for the Winter & takes one at Hastings whither with all the family of the Jenkinsons remove by the 1st of - *[no month given]*
	Alveston let to Mr Holder of Birmingham.

December 12	Charles goes to Town for three nights - sends his eldest son Charles[1] to the Jenkinson at Hastings for his health - attended the Chester House Meeting[2] - calls at Richmond on good old Dr G Wollaston in his way to Bushy Park[3] - the seat of the Duke of Clarence, where he sleeps …
14	…on the following day he writes me a most pleasing letter with an account of the very flattering manner in which he is received by the Duke & Duchess & of his having agreed to take Mr Fitzclarence as his pupil - who tho' now a sailor, is to be fitted for the Church. Charles likewise communicates to me the intelligence of poor Mr Freeman's death at Mezieres in France in the end of last month & that the Estates of Fawley devolve on Admiral Perre Williams[4] - a man of 83.
21	My Sister writes me word of her having seen a letter from William Fanshawe announcing his marriage with M[lle] Meisner as having taken place last October - he writes from Warsaw whither my Brother is expected after visiting his Polish Estate.

---

[1] Charles Fanshawe (1806-1873) suffered from Asthma all his life.
[2] Meetings revolved around the differences between Wesleyans & Primitive Methodists.
[3] George III appointed his son the Duke of Clarence, the Ranger of Bushy Park during 1797 and subsequently Clarence made Bushy House his home with his mistress Dorothea Jordan and their ten children. Their relationship ended in 1811 but the children continued living at Bushy Park with their father and were joined by Princess Adelaide in 1818 after her marriage to Clarence.
[4] Admiral of the Fleet William Peere Williams-Freeman (1742-1832) whose maternal grandmother was Mary Freeman, sister of John Cook Freeman of Fawley Court. As his two sons predeceased the Admiral, the heir to Fawley Court was his surviving grandson.

1821
Events public.

January	Attempts in the House of Commons for the restoration of the Queen's name in the Liturgy by the Opposition, but [rejected] completely by Ministry who on this & every question seem very completely to carry their point - and even the commonest of the people it is to be hoped - open their eyes to the unworthiness of the Queen.
	£50,000 p^r ann - voted as her provision for life.
February	It is reported the Queen refuses to accept her pension.
March	Her Majesty <u>condescends.</u>
May & June	The Queen's party are not ashamed to make as indecent speeches in the House as she herself can desire.
July	Parliament prorogued 'till Autumn.
	Queen asserts her claim to be crowned with the King - as Queen of England - is refused.
19	Magnificent Coronation[1] of the King in proper form - at which the Queen attempts to be admitted as a common spectator, coming to the Gate of Westminster Abbey, knocks at the door & is refused. After the day - sends an absurd as well as insolent demand to the King - to have a separate Coronation to herself on the Monday following - is refused & informs the King she intends visiting Scotland in the course of the Summer, whither it was supposed he - intended going himself after his return from

---

[1] 19th July - George VI famed for extravagance, commissiond a new crown for his Coronation at a cost of £230,000 - set with 12,000 diamonds it is known as the 'George IV State Diadem'.

	Ireland!!
21	King sails from Portsmouth on his intended visit to Ireland.
August 3	Queen[1] very seriously ill & on the 4th - in considerable danger.
7	Death[2] of the Queen.
	[3]Dreadful riots in London on the removal of the Queen's body for interment out of England & the mob offer the greatest insult to the soldiers who attend the Procession. One man killed by the firing of the soldiers to protect themselves from the stones & mud which they were scandalously pelted during this endeavour to guard a passage for the hearse - which was at length safely shipped off for the Continent & the Queen buried at Brunswick.
	The King received in the most magnificent & loyal manner in Ireland[4].
September	Returns to England after a very boistrous passage from Dublin[5] to the Welsh coast & arrives to London on the 15th. Sets out again in a few days for a tour of the Continent & sails from Ramsgate to Calais where he is received with the greatest acclaimation & respect - proceeds to Hanover.
October	Returns to England in - *[no month]*
November	Parliament prorogued 'till the beginning of next year.
December	Dreadfully riotous disturbances in Ireland.
	Parliament again prorogued 'till February.

---

[1] Caroline, uncrowned Queen and estranged wife of George IV.
[2] Queen Caroline died at Hammersmith aged 53.
[3] 25th August - funeral at Brunwick, Germany.
[4] 12th August - arrived at West Pier in Howth.
[5] 3rd September - departed from Dunleary aboard the Royal Yacht.

| December | Towards the end of the month most violent storms of wind & rain[1] are productive of infinite mischief both by sea & land throughout the Kingdom. |

Queen Caroline's funeral procession

---

[1] Significant flooding along the Thames during December & January resulting from excess rainfall in the second-half of 1821 - floods were reported at Henley, Maidenhead & Kingston-upon-Thames.

1822
Family marriages, deaths or births.

		Marriages	Deaths	Births
July	Mrs Moody[1] a girl.			—
August	Mrs Trevor a boy[2]			—

> **Memory**
> …The affectation of correct memory shews itself by knowing, to the precise exactitude of a day, the date of the birth, marriage, or deah of any one who is named… AF

---

[1] 6th October (christened) - Robert Sadleir Moody (1822-1907) at St Peter's Church South Weald.
[2] 31st July - Althea Mary Trevor died 1847 in the East Indies - [AF obviously made errors in reversing the sexes of these two children].

1822
Marriages, deaths or Births among acquaintances or neighbours.

		Marriages	Deaths	Births
March	Mr Atkyns Wright[1] of Crowsley Park.		—	
	Doctor Parry[2]		—	
	Sir Henry Englefield[3]		—	
	General Donkin[4]		—	
May	Mrs Lysaght[5] of the Circus		—	
July	Rev[d] Edward Townshend[6] of Bray & Henley		—	

---

[1] 5th March - John Atkyns-Wright - according to 'the Diaries of Mrs Philip Lybbe Powys of Hardwick House', Mrs Atkyns Wright and AF's mother Mrs Althea Fanhsawe were both in the intimate circle of neighbourly friends at Shiplake. Mrs Mary Wright had come to live at Crowsley Park in 1790 and died three years after, her property passed to her nephew John Atkins who by 1796 had assumed the name Atkyns-Wright - his widow died in 1842.

[2] 9th March - Dr Caleb Hiller Parry buried in Bath Abbey where members of the medical profession in Bath commissioned a monument to his memory.

[3] 21st March - Sir Henry Charles Englefield, 7th Baronet FRS FRSE FSA FLS (1752-1822) English antiquary and astronomer was born at Englefield House, Reading. In 1780 he inherited from his father his estate at nearby Earley, called Whiteknights Park in addition to the Engelfield estates at Wootton Bassett, Wiltshire. He was unmarried and dying without an heir, his title became extinct.

[4] 6th March - General Robert Donkin born 1727 died at Bristol after army service lasting 80 years - his death recorded in the Gentleman's Magazine 1822.

[5] 3rd May - Honourable Henrietta Lysaght died aged 68 - widow of Hon Joseph Lysaght and daughter of St. Leger St. Leger, 1st Viscount Doneraile and Mary Barry.

[6] 24th July - extract of obituary in 'The Christian Observer' …'*died the Reverend Edward Townshend, 33 years Vicar of Bray, Berks & Rector of Henley-on-Thames 38 years. He was the only son of the Honourable and Reverend Edward Townshend, Dean of Norwich, who married Mary, daughter of General Price. Being deprived of his father while young, he was received into the family of his uncle, the Honourable and Most Reverend Dr. Cornwallis, Archbishop of Canterbury, with whom he resided until he went to college….*'

	Mr Martin Annesley[1] of Reading		—	
December	Mr Phinn[2] to Miss Litchfield	—		

*General Robert Donkin 1727-1821
- 'in the Pump-Room at Bath 1809'.*

---

[1] 28th June - died at Reading - Alderman Martin Annesley, born 1740.
[2] 10th December - Thomas Phinn, the Apothacary, widowed the previous October, married Jane Litchfield at Walcot.

1822
Family events & circumstances relative to myself.

January	Charles makes me a visit of five days & leaves me on the 12th.
March	Great increase of illness.
May 6	Out for first time since last October in a wheel chair.
June	Very ill indeed & considerably hurt by a fall on the ground during a fit.
July	Illness of every kind increases & suffer greatly from rheumatism, strange cold seizures & extreme weakness - cannot get out even in a wheel chair.
August	Somewhat mended - out once or twice.
	Uncomfortably disappointed of an expected visit from Charles towards the end of the month, by the loss of a letter.
September	Greatly hurt by bruises on my face & throat, owing to a fall on the ground during a fit - followed by a great number of fits for several days & then by illness of every kind exactly in the same manner as that in July.
October	Out twice only in the wheel chair - on the 3rd & 4th of the month after which, all going out was given up at least for the year! Illness of all sorts considerably increasing - my eyes in particular very much injured by the fall of the preceeding month.

November	A letter from Mr Drummond gives me notice of a distribution of £1.5s per share on 90 London Assurance[1], having been received by him for me amounting to £112.10s.
December	Charles makes me a five days visit quite at the end of the year, which I conclude with great increase of illness.

Fits 44 - Attacks 67

Fireman's Arm Badge - 1801
The London Assurance Company

---

[1] AF's cousin Henry S. H Wollaston (1776-1867) was listed as a director of the London Assurance from 1817 onwards.

1822
Events private.

January	Charles informs me of his legacy from the late Mr Freeman of £500 - on the 16th goes to Hastings to fetch his son Charles away from the Jenkinsons - finds him much improved in health & their family in the usual sick & dissatisfied state!
February	A great deal of illness in the Jenkinson family; John Jenkinson[1] parts with his commission in the Guards & the present scheme is for him to take Orders when it can be determined in which of the universities he shall prosecute his studies!
	Charles's new pupil Mr Augustus Fitzclarance[2] now with him.
March	John Jenkinson[3] entered in Magdalen Hall, Oxford.
April	Charles administers the Sacrament at Bushy & is greatly pleased by the proper behaviour of the Duke & Duchess & his own gracious reception.
June	Jenkinsons return to Alveston or rather to the neighbourhood for the house itself is painting & they live for the time in their gardeners… Sophie is to pass the summer at Cheltenham for the use of the waters & Dr Boisragon's[4] advice.

---

[1] Rev'd John Simon Jenkinson (1798-1871) Vicar of Battersea.
[2] Lord Augustus FitzClarence (1805-1854) the youngest illegitimate son of the Duke of Clarence (William IV) and his long-time mistress Dorothea Jordan.
[3] 14th March - matriculated Magdalen Hall, Oxford.
[4] Dr Boisragon moved his practice from Bath to Cheltenham prior to 1814 and became extremely successful. With a practice in Royal Crescent, he was also appointed Physician Extrordinaire to George, Prince of Wales.

	Measles[1] disturbingly prevalent in Charles's family but all get thro' it very well.
August	Charles's Fitzclarence pupil runs away from Fawley & he is greatly dissatisfied, but find him at his sister's in London.
	Miss Catherine Fanshawe after a three years visit to Italy again returns to her sisters.
	Sophia Jenkinson also leaves Cheltenham for her father's house at Alveston.
	Mr Hay once more seized with his old Continental <u>travelling disorder</u>!
September	Sophia Jenkinson again ill & returns to Cheltenham for Dr Boisragon's advice, my Sister goes with her but knows not for how long.
November	Poor Mrs Charles Fanshawe in very great danger from an alarming inward complaint to which she has often been subject but never had so bad a seizure - that of which Charles gave me notice on the 7th of the month - in about ten days, safe as to life but still in a very precarious state - by the end of the month is called recovered but very weak & is said to be in a family way.
December	Jenkinsons at length determine to pass their Winter at Cheltenham where they hire a house - No. 2 Montague Place from this time 'tll the month of May of next year.

---

[1] Measles symptoms include fever, cough, runny nose, inflamed eyes and a rash and it is very contagious. Since a vaccine was discovered in 1963, a well-maintained vaccination programme keeps a check on this illness.

1822
Events public.

January	Dreadful proceedings amongst the Irish rioters.
February	Habeas Corpus Act suspended that relative to Insurrections put in force <u>that is not forcible!</u>
April	Riots in Ireland said to be in some measure subdued, yet still dreadful & the distress from want of food in some parts of the Kingdom very great indeed.
August	After a long & laborious session, Parliament is at last prorogued on the 8th by the King in person 'till the 8th of next October.
	On the 10th - the King embarks at Greenwich for his long intended visit to Scotland which after a very tempestuous voyage of four days he reached on the 14th[1]. Was received in Edinburgh with grand rejoicings & returned to London by a much quicker passage than he went - being only 72 hours on board the yacht.
	On the 12th of this eventful month, Lord Londonderry[2], a Prime Minister, in a fit of insanity… produced as it is said by over exertion & fatigue during the late quarrelsome session, destroys himself

---

[1] George IV arrived in the *'Royal George'* in Firth of Forth on Wednesday 14th August. This was the irst time the monarch had visited Scotland in 200 years. Landing was postponed due to torrential rain but Sir Walter Scott and his Waverley novels had so impressed the King and the Scots, his 'reinvention' of the traditions and kilts of Scotland would not be put off. Scott was rowed out to the King - who exclaimed, "What! Sir Walter Scott! The man in Scotland I most wish to see!"

[2] AF's comments at the time reflect much that has been written since about this tragic situation - it is generally assumed that Lord Castlereagh (Lord Londonderry) acted at a result of work-induced depression and paranoia - *'No British statesman of the 19th century reached the same level of international influence….But very few have been so maligned by their own countrymen and so abused in history. This shy and handsome Ulsterman is perhaps the most hated domestic political figure in both modern British and Irish political history'* (his biographer John Bew).

	by cutting his throat with a penknife! The confusion both in public & private life consequent on so shocking a misfortune is of course immense.
September	Mr Canning succeeds Ld Londonderry as a Prime Minister.[1]
November	Parliament prorogues to February is the following year.

Rt. Hon. George Canning, MP (1770-1827)
After Thomas Lawrence - c1820
National Trust Collections

---

[1] 16th September 1822 - Lord Londonderry, the Foreign Secretary was succeeded by George Canning.

1823
Family marriages, deaths or births.

		Marriages	Deaths	Births
January	Henry Fanshawe[1] to Miss Caroline Luttrell	—		
February	Commissioner Fanshawe[2] at the great age of 83		—	
April	Mr Luttrell[3] father of Mrs F.		—	
May	Sophia Jenkinson[4] of a deep decline		—	
June 18	Mrs C Fanshawe a boy William[5]			—
August 25	William Fanshawe[6]		—	
	Henry Jenkinson[7] to Miss Elizabeth Acland	—		
September 21	Mrs C Fanshawe[8]		—	
October 11	Francis John Hyde Wollaston[1] - the Archdeaon died suddenly at his		—	

---

[1] 20th January - Capt. Henry Fanshawe RN to Caroline Luttrell at St Marylebone, Westminster.
[2] 4th February - Capt. Robert Fanshawe (1740-1823) at Plymouth.
[3] 24th April - Francis Fownes Luttrell (1756-1823) MP for Minehead (1780-1783), Commissioner for Taxes, and later Customs - before being the chair of the Board of Customs (1813-1819).
[4] 27th May (burial) - Sophia Jenkinson aged 31 at Cheltenham.
[5] William Faithfull Fanshawe - last son of Charles & Patty Fanshawe was born at Clarges Street, London, where he died a few weeks later.
[6] 27th August (burial) at St George's Hanover Square.
[7] 25th August - Capt. Henry Jenkinson married Elizabeth Lucy Theresa, youngest daughter of the late Sir Thomas Dyke Acland, Bart., M.P. for North Devon.
[8] Patty (Faithfull) Fanshawe.
[1] 12th October - died in his sleep at the house of his brother William Hyde Wollaston.

	brother's in Town			
December	Both my Brother's Russian daughters-in-law, the wives of William[1] & Frederic[2] - of a son.			— —

Spencer jacket worn by Elizabeth Acland for her marriage to Henry Fanshawe (August 1823)

---

[1] Henry Constantine Fanshawe (1823-1853).
[2] Henry Constantine Fanshawe (1822-1886) - later Lt General Russian Army.

1823
Marriages, deaths or Births among acquaintances or neighbours.

		Marriages	Deaths	Births
January	Lady Macclesfield[1]		—	
	Mrs Daubery of the Crescent		—	
	Mrs Walmesley[2] of the Circus		—	
February	Lady Johnson[3] of Catherine Place		—	
	Miss Maude[4] - of Marlborough Buildings		—	
	Mr Lutwyche[5] D[d].		—	
	Rev[d] Mr Cobbe[6] - D[d] suddenly at his mother's house - was to be married in a few days!		—	
May	Mrs Gage[7] - Paragon Buildings		—	

---

[1] 1st January - Mary Frances, Countess of Macclesfield (1761-1823), formerly Mary Drake, and wife of George Parker, 4th Earl of Macclesfield was Lady of the Bedchamber to Queen Charlotte. She died at Shirburn Castle.

[2] 23rd January - Mary, daughter of William Cunliffe Shawe of Singleton, Lancs & wife of John Walmesley, died at 78 - buried at Bath Abbey.

[3] 13th February - Rebecca Franks died aged 63, born in America was a British loyalist in the American Revolution married to Lt. Henry Johnson (later General Sir) in command of the British Garrison at Stony Point, New York - in 1779 they were forced to flee to England.

[4] 26th February - Miss Sophia Maud, aged 63.

[5] 23rd February - William Lutwyche, aged 78.

[6] 23rd March - Henry William Cobbe (1785-1823) Vicar of Templeton and son of Charles Cobbe an Irish politician.

[7] 5th June - Mrs Sidney Gage of 12 Paragon Buildings Bath died aged 95.

	Lady Vernon[1]		—	
June	Mr John Bowdler[2] Esq[r] - brother to my friend.		—	
August	Lady Palliser[3] - suddenly		—	
	Miss Caroline Parry[4] the daughter of my late friend Dr P to Mr Martineau	—		
November	Mrs Keene formerly Miss Ruch		—	
	Frederic Faithfull[5] - brother of the late Mrs Charles Fanshawe in India		—	

Jane Georgiana Fauquier Venables Vernon
by John Hoppner c1785-1800
(detail from a full portrait)

---

[1] 31st May - Jane Georgiana Venables (1746-1823) daughter of William Fauquier & 2nd wife of George Venables-Vernon died 1813.

[2] 29th June - John Bowdler (1746-1823) died at Eltham - a campaigner for moral reform and a founder of the Church Building Society.

[3] 5th August - Mary, Lady Palliser widow of Sir Hugh Palliser 2nd Bt (1768-1813) and daughter of John Gates of Dedham Essex.

[4] 2nd September - Caroline Parry married Joseph Martineau, son of a Norwich doctor. Described on his death in 1863 as a wealthy landowner, he acquired Basing Park Estate in 1836 & created an outstanding garden with many evergreen trees, shrubs, rose and rock gardens, a walled kitchen garden, and an arboretum - the house was in the style of a Grecian Temple.

[5] 11th December - Frederick Faithfull (1787-1823) - officer of the East India Co., died in Bombay, India.

1823
Family events & circumstances relative to myself.

January	Charles leaves me on the 4th after a five day visit.
	Mrs Charles still very ill, they go to Town for advice & then soon after their return she is seized wth a violent increase of the same terrible complaint from which she suffered so much last year & for the whole of the month.
February	Continues in a sad state confined to bed without much hope of amendment, yet is said to be in no danger.
March & April	Much in the same state throughout both months, poor Sophia Jenkinson keeps time on the invalid list! - to the great affliction of all the family who still continue at Cheltenham
May	- 'till in the month of May she is at length released after a long & hopeless decline - on the 22nd.
	Give Charles £100.
	Out for the first time since last October in a wheel chair, on the 2nd of this month.
June	Very increasingly ill in every way.
July	A two day visit ending on the first from Charles who brings sad account of his poor wife.
	Give Charles £2400 out of the sale of £3000 red-ann - producing when sold £2497.10.-
August	After long confinement get out for the first time in a chair.
September & October	A fortnight of violently increased illness - remake my Will in consequence of poor Mrs Charles Fanshawe's death - leaving all I have to him.
	Mr Hay, Mr Phinn & Mr Church are witnesses to it.

	Receive a very pleasing visit from Capt. H Jenkinson & his bride[1] in their way thro' Bath.
28	See without difficulty from my window the ascent of the Balloon[2] from a yard near the Bristol Road which fell again in about an hour & which all Bath crowded the fields to behold.
November 17	Having destroyed the duplicate of the former Will (which I have received from Mr Fane) I have now given the duplicate of my present Will into the care of Mr Hay.
December	Charles make me a visit quite at the end of the year which I conclude with somewhat less illness than I have of late suffered.

Fits 37 - Attacks 47

Central transfer of a "Balloon" patterned vegetable dish issued to commemorate Graham's Balloon flight

---

[1] 25th August - at Broadclyst, Devon, Capt. Henry Jenkinson of Alveston Warwickshire married Elizabeth Lucy Theresa Acland daughter of Thomas Dyke-Acland.

[2] George Graham was becoming established as an early balloonist. The failure of this flight was found to be due to blocked gas pipes and the following year, after moving his balloon to another location in Bath, with his wife Margaret Graham (1804-1864) they achieved success. Mrs Graham, born at Walcot Bath, was a very able manager of her husband's spectacular career, and also by making the first of her several solo flight in 1826, she is acknowledged as the first British solo woman balloonist.

1823
Events private.

February	By the death of an uncle, Mr Drewe[1] - Henry Fanshawe's wife comes into a legacy of £1500 and an equal sum is left to each of her three sisters as likewise, to eight other relations by the same old gentleman.
April	Mr Luttrell[2], father to Mrs Fanshawe dies after long illness - my Sister says her fortune is £6000.
	The Jenkinsons change their house in Cheltenham where they mean to remain as long as poor Sophia still lives.
May - June	On the 22nd the poor sufferer is released.
	Mrs C F before her expected time lays in of a boy.
August 2	Charles carries his poor wife for advice in London, where they are in the house of the Miss Strickland's - N° 6 Clariges Street. Charles is called back to Fawley by the illness of the children owing to Whooping Cough. Mrs C continues very bad but he hopes in a few days to remove her to the comforts of home.
25	- the little William is released, which is indeed a blessing in their sad state.
	The marriage in the Jenkinson family of Capt H Jenkinson, their eldest son to Miss Acland, a very amiable woman of good family & bringing him a considerable fortune of £17000 - 3p^r. ann - makes them very happy & happens at a fortunate time… rather to raise upwards much lowered by late annuities.

---

[1] William Drewe (1745-1821) of New Street, Spring Gardens, Westminster, a lawyer of New Inn, London who died unmarried.
[2] 24th April - Francis Fownes-Luttrell (1756-1823), Commissioner of Cutoms.

August 28	Charles has the comfort of bringing his poor wife back in safety to their own dear home, not the worse but not I fear the better for them. Long medical consultation which after all ends in little more than information that such cases have <u>sometimes</u> been known to be recovered! A discovery that it needed not the consultation of these wise men to inform one of…
September 21	After dreadful sufferings poor Mrs C F is at length released from misery in this world to I hope & trust happiness in the next! Her death was at last, as one may term it <u>sudden</u> for Charles actually thought her just dropped off to sleep when she expired in his arms! A medical man who had seen her as late as four o'clock, said there was no imminent danger yet the event took place at eleven that very evening!
October	The extremely sudden death of the Archdeacon Wollaston[1], the eldest brother of that extremely large family, was a great shock to them all - but particularly so to his brother Dr W to whose house in Town he arrived on the eve, appeared quite well 'till bed time & the following morning was found dead by the servant who went to call him - the fit which carried him off is supposed to have been of an Epileptic nature.

---

[1] 1st November - Francis Hyde John Wollaston, Archdeaon of Essex, who with his family lived at the Vicarage, South Weald, Essex.

October	Charles Simon Faithfull Fanshawe[1] fixed at Oxford - Magdelen College.
November	Fanny Jenkinson having been for some time very ill <u>in the old way</u>, is for the present called well & brought home by my Sister to enjoy the pleasures of house full of relations at Alveston, where both Capt. & Mrs Fanshawe & Capt & Mrs H Jenkinson now are & my Sister writes in good spirits.
December	A visit from Henry Fanshawe & his wife to Fawley where they pass a week, gives Charles the greatest pleasure finding as he does that his **Sister-in-law[2] is a Sister in deed & a very amiable woman - her kind behaviour too, to his daughter is particularly satisfactory to him.

> ** Note recordred in original diary by H C Fanshawe
> *'she proved to be an absolute angel to them'*

---

[1] 26th July 1823 - at sixteen, the eldest son of AF's nephew Charles matriculated from Magdalen College, Oxford. Then intent on a BA, awarded in 1827, he gained his MA in 1830. Later that year he was ordained and made chaplain to Lord Glentworth before succeeding his father as Rector of Fawley on 22 December 1832. He married Rosetta Maynard Ricketts in 1833 who in later years, became the close friend of the writer William Makepeace Thackeray.

[2] Henry Fanshawe's 2nd wife Caroline, whom he had married in January that year.

1823
Events public.

February	Parliament meets at the appointed time but the King is too ill to make his speech himself, which is read[1] by Commission.
	Comes to Town once on business but returns to Brighton - still bad with the gout.
March - April	Tho' returned to London, strangely & mysteriously ill - remove to Windsor on the end of…
July	Parliament on 16th prorogued 'till the end of September - the King's speech by commission.
August	Spanish & French disturbances[2] & strange proceedings - too completely puzzled at all to comprehend the reports with which newspapers overflow.
	Death of the old Pope Pius 8th[3] aged 84 at Rome.
September - October	King of Spain released from his captivity at Cadiz.

---

[1] 4th February - the King's speech was read by the Lord Chancellor.
[2] To maintain stability in Europe, the Congress System was introduced following the Napoleonic Wars. This allowed the Congress of Verona to authorize France to intervene during 1822 when a liberal government in Spain came into trouble. King Louis XVIII of France responded by sending a massive army in April 1823 which met little Spanish resistance and King Ferdinand was re-installed as an absolute monarch.
[3] 30th November - at Quirinal Palace, Rome.

1824
Family marriages, deaths or births.

		Marriages	Deaths	Births
April 20	Miss Althea Fanshawe		—	
	[above entry in the original diary by H C Fanshawe]			

Gratitude

This, which is one of the most delightful feelings of the human mind, seems so natural, as for it to be impossible ever to affect that which without any effort, belongs to every being that exists. It is exerted towards our fellow-creatures from the moment of our birth, and gives double pleasure to every kindness we receive; it is in the most exalted manner constantly directed to the Giver of all good, in whom we live, we move, and have our being! Gratitude begins our morning, gratitude concludes our night; every instant of the day, and every object it presents, calls forth and loves its Maker.... AF

1824

Marriages, deaths or Births among acquaintances or neighbours.

		Marriages	Deaths	Births
January	Mrs L Grote of Badgemore[1]		—	
February	Mr Fane[2] of Wormsley		—	
	Mrs Fountain of the Crescent		—	

---

[1] Connected to the London banking family of Grote & Prescott.
[2] 8th February - John Fane DCL (1751-1824) of Wormsley, Tory MP for Oxfordshire for the parliaments of 1796, 1802, 1806, 1807, 1812, 1818, and 1820.

1824
Family events & circumstances relative to myself.

January	Charles leaves me on the 8th after a ten days visit.
February	Extreme illness of various sorts in addition to the old story!
29	A letter from my brother dated Jan 9 from Petersburgh surprises me not a little after a silence of three years (April 1821) this letter is jointly to my Sister & myself to give notice of his son George's approaching marriage with a Polish lady a Mlle Bonnet[1].

---

[1] 11 May - married at Warsaw Louise Bonnet de Bélon (1802-1876) - Mlle Bonnet was French *(ref HFF)*.

1824
Events private.

| February | Charles again undertakes the care of his runaway pupil Augustus Fitzclarence[1] & is pleased by a letter from the Duke. |

Lord Augustus FitzClarence (1805-1854)

---

[1] For how long Fitzclarence remained with Charles Fanshawe is not known but the time spent proved successful - Fanshawe continued in the favour of the Royal couple and Fitzclarence settled to a religious calling. In 1828, he married Sarah, daughter of Major Lord Henry Gordon, and in 1829 was appointed Chaplain to his father. The following year he was presented as Vicar of Mapledurham, Oxon.

Althea Fanshawe died on the 24th April 1824 and consequently there are no further entries in the diary completed by Althea.

However, in the course of the preparation of the History of the Fanshawe Family, this diary came into the possession of history's author H.C. Fanshawe and at that time he made several notes and observations on the unused pages of the diary and marked entries that particularly interested him.

To avoid confusion, we have not included any of these notes as most have been incorporated either in the family history or within the biographical information contained in this publication.

In the case of historical interest we have included the following letters kept within the diary - they indicate the interest shown by various members of the family through whose hands the diary passed.

A3 & A4

(Letter inserted)

> 14 Ch[rist] Ch[urch] Road
>
> November 30

My dear Herbert

     I think you may like to have this old family book, so I am sending it to you as you will make more use of it than we should. The lady seems to have had very poor health - in 1816 she says she had 327 attacks and 30 fits which left her little leisure for anything else. We are unfortunately without a servant, ours having collapsed with influenza on Tuesday - so have not been getting much rest. A maid is coming on Monday.

Mother would have been 86 yesterday - this time last year she was quite able to enjoy life - now she enjoys the fuller life…

We rather think of putting on the grave "Venus stood on the shore" - a very favourite text of hers.

> Yr affectionate cousin
>
> (Edith or Eizh) Hoare[1]
>
> *(poems see XXII - 183)*

---

[1] Maria Faithfull Fanshawe the youngest sister of the father of H C Fanshawe married Revd Arthur Malortie Hoare in 1853.

A5 & A6

Book Plate at End

I have not begun this with any degree of sanity till a year & four months after our mother's death. I am determined on it as I can, to make out the deficiency of this time by recollection, & for the future keep up her custom of noting all family occurrences & such amongst my acquaintance & public facts as may happen to take me. Death & marriages of acquaintance is certainly particularly convenient to write down as it is sometime very useful to <u>happen</u> to know when any <u>happened</u> which are a sort <u>I</u> almost constantly forget.

1806 - May 13

(mother died 1st Jan 1805 - p4)

Note written to H C Fanshawe

This diary was given me by my aunt Mrs Hoare (Maria Faithfull Fanshawe) to whom it came from her sister Miss Susannah Frances F.F. it came (after) from the widow of Adm. Hy. Fanshawe[1] of Tillwater, Godstone

1906

(over)

See comparison of the diary with that of her sister Mrs John Jenkinson[2] (M.O.S. book III 71-6)

---

[1] Eldest nephew of Althea Fanshawe & son of General Henry Fanshawe (Russian Service).
[2] AF's sister Frances Fanshawe (1760-1830).

Appendix 1

Henry Fanshawe of Dengie & Martin

(1756 – 1828)

Extract from

The History of The Fanshawe Family

by

H.C. Fanshawe

Publisher: Andrew Reid & Company
1927

History of The Fanshawe Family – Pages 277 -279

'The third successor of the Dengie Branch of the Fanshawes of Parsloes and the sixth in descent from William Fanshawe, founder of that house, was Henry Fanshawe, who like his father and grandfather was an only son when he succeeded.

He was born on 5th May 1756, and died in Warsaw, a General in the Russian Service and Senator, on 25th February 1828.

He was the first of the family who was educated at Eton, where he was from 1766 to 1770, rising to the Fifth form in the latter year, in which he was gazetted as Ensign in the 1st Foot Guards on 4 October. He was promoted to be Lieutenant in 1776 (these two commission costing his father £600 and £900), and later to be adjutant; part of the time he was attached to the company of his cousin, Colonel West Hyde. In May 1781 he became Captain on payment of £5000 for his commission; but not long afterwards he retired from the Guards and was appointed Lt. Col. Of the 83rd Regiment., then mustering in Guernsey; meanwhile on 24 February, 1778, a year after the death of his father, he had married Susanna Frances, second daughter and coheiress of Charles Le Grys and his wife Elizabeth Bladwell of Morton on the Hill or Helmingham, eight miles north of Norwich, and their eldest son Henry, was born at Shiplake in his grandmother's house on 9 November or December in the same year.

Their second son Charles Robert, grandfather of the present compiler, was born on 4th April 1780, and a third son Thomas Edward on 9th May 1781; both of these were baptised in St James' Westminster (26 April 1780 & 23 May 1781). The younger boy died as a boy of 16 in South Russia in October 1797.

By his marriage settlement of 18 February 1778, a jointure of £400 p.a. was secured to his wife on the Dengie &

Martin estates, subject to his mother's jointure of £500p.a; and his aunt Miss Anna Snelling placed £12,000 in the hands of three trustees – The Reverend Francis Wollaston of the Charterhouse, John Fanshawe of Shabden, and Robert Palmer – for payment of the interest thereon to her nephew after her death…'

After follows details of the events that lead to Henry Fanshawe joining the Russian Service – as already explained.

<u>Continues : H of FF – Pages 279 –287</u>

'…Colonel Fanshawe proceeded to St Petersburg in May 1784, and soon after his arrival there, was appointed by the Empress Catherine to the command of a Russian Regt. in the Crimea. His wife and three children meanwhile, returning to her mother at Norwich (the second boy Charles Robert having remained in England with his paternal grandmother and aunt).

In the October of the following year he became Colonel of the Ekaterinoslavak: Jaferski Regt., and his wife rejoined him with their eldest and two youngest sons, a fifth son, Frederick George was born to them at Cherson on 6/17 March 1788, a sixth son George, at St.in May 1791. Their only little girl had a brief life of a single month.

The record of Henry Fanshawe's services, obtained before 1914 from the *The General Archives of the Army Staff*[1] show that his Regt. distinguished itself in the Bug campaign of 1787-8, and especially at the battle of Ochakov and the Liman, and that its Colonel received the Order of (the Great Martyr) St George, 4th grade, and the Golden Sword for distinguished valour in action. He served in this campaign

---

[1] These official documents give a list of the orders of which the 4 Fanshawe. Generals were Knights and a detailed account of their services in the Russian army, and of Frederick Fanshawe's Diplomatic career.

under Prince Potemkin (of whom he wrote 37 years later that he, the Prince, had always been his protector, and that after his death – which occurred in Bessarabia on 16 October 1791 – he had suffered much from the caprices of the Russian Court, in which it was very difficult to keep clear of intrigues and steer the right road); he served also under General Suvarov, and no doubt met the famous Admiral Paul Jones, who was in command of the sea fleet at Ochakov. The above Archives record Henry Fanshawe's Knighthood.

On 4 November 1788, he wrote a most interesting narrative of the siege of this place to General Conway, from which the following account is taken. The river flotilla under the Prince of Nassau Siegen was arranged in five divisions, first bomb ketches and fire rafts, second floating batteries, third 12 cutters armed with howitzers, fourth, under Colonel Fanshawe, seven galleys of 54 banks of oars, armed with howitzers and 3-pounders, and protected by gun boats with 18-pounders, and fifth 5 Barcassen (long boats) with 18^{in} howitzers. Early in May the fleet moved from Cherson to be ready for the siege on the arrival of the army under Prince Potemkin, and while lying off Kimburn (at the end of a long spit on the south side of the estuary of the Duieper, and due south of the mouth of the Bug and of Ochakov on the west bank) was surprised on 19th May by the unexpected arrival of the famous Turkish Admiral Hasan Pasha with a force of 4 ships of the line, 11 frigates and some 14 smaller craft, to which the Russians could oppose only 2 men of war, 2 frigates and 8 small vessels. After various slight skirmishes a more considerable one took place on 6-7th June, the Turks losing 5-6 small craft; and at 1pm on the 18th the Capitan Pasha advanced for a general engagement, his own ship standing directly against the Vladimer, the flagship of Paul

Jones. The narrowness of the channel of approach compelled the Turks to tack repeatedly, and about 5pm the Pasha's ship ran aground, and the advance stopped.

During the night, a Russian Council of War decided to attack the Turkish fleet at daybreak, and the Russian men of war and gunboats and 4 galleys did so. After half an hour's cannonade the enemy fell back under the guns of Ochakov, two men of war going aground, one of them the Turkish flagship. These were attacked, the galleys taking a prominent part in the attack as their commander did not consider himself to be under the orders of the Sea Admiral (Henry Fanshawe received the Order of St. Ann for the action), and one was burnt by her crew. The flagship after some treacherous behaviour of the company was surrendered, but a fire subsequently broke out on her, and she also perished by the flames.

Three days later the gunboats and galleys were sent out to destroy a number of other vessels which had become stranded during the Turkish retreat, and a smart engagement of five hours ensued, nineteen being killed and wounded on Colonel Fanshawe's own galley. Among the latter was his son Henry, a lad of 9 years age only, who was acting as a midshipman and who was wounded in the head by a splinter. One Turkish line of battle ships and 3 frigates were destroyed on this occasion.

On 22 June Prince Potemkin arrived at the fleet and hoisted his flag as Admiral of the Fleet in the Black & Caspian Seas on board Col. Fanshawe's galley, in which he subsequently proceeded to reconnoitre the fortress of Ochakov.

Five days later the army arrived before it, consisting of 32 battalions, 72 squadrons and 60 heavy guns, and on 1st

July, made an abortive attack on the place supported by a heavy fire from the fleet which drove the defenders on the sea front from the outworks, Ochakov was then gradually invested.

Colonel Fanshawe condemns very strongly the dilatoriness and supineness of the Russian commanders during the siege, which resulted in terrible sufferings to the army, and the loss of half its strength and the complete destruction of the calvary regts. On one occasion in November the Turks captured and killed the Officer of the day, General Maximovitch and hung his head over the wall. About this time Admiral Paul Jones threw up his command in disgust – he had been on very bad terms throughout with the Prince of Nassau Siegen.

At last, on the 6 December, the day of St. Nicholas, a general assault was made by the whole remaining Russian force now reduced to 14,000 effectives, and this proved successful. For while the Turks concentrated wholly against the right assault, which they bravely held up, the left wing made its way in practically unopposed, and the enemy, taken between the two forces, was simply annihilated. Col. Fanshawe states their loss at 8,000. Anthing[1] in his 'Campaigns of Suvarov', at 15,000. The scene of the capture must have been as terrible as that of Ismail 2 years later, of which Lord Byron gives so lurid a picture in Canto VIII of Don Juan: Anthing says, *"Ceux qui avaient assiégé Ochakov et qui estoient à Ismail ne mettoient aucune comparison entre les deux sieges"*. Col. Fanshawe puts the Russian loss on the capture at 3,000, and the total loss at 18,000. Anthing gives 4,800 for the former. Castera in his *'History of Catherine II'*

---

[1] Johann Friedrich Anthing (1753–1805) German artist and historian who became Marshal Alexander Suvorov's Aide-de-camp.

states that the total Russian loss was 20,000 and the Turkish loss 25,000. He also records that the Prince of Nassau's victory was due principally to the courage and talents of two French Officers, "the Englishman Fanshawe and the Dutchman Winter". The reward received by Col. Fanshawe has already been noted – his young son was appointed "an officer in the (Russian) Navy without examination which at nine years of age was impossible and could not be done but by particular order of her Majesty to dispense with it".

In July of the year after Ochakov we have (in *Swinton's Travels*) a glimpse in peace surroundings at Ingria near Cronstadt (1792). The writer was aroused by martial music and rose to see marching past, a Regt. of *"a very fine body of men, all dressed in white jackets and trousers of linen for the convenience of marching in such sultry weather. Colonel Fanshawe arrived some days since with his family. His little son not exceeding ten years of age has already bled in the field of Mars. He was wounded at the siege of Ochakov. His father takes him with him in all his expeditions".*

In 1789-90 Colonel Fanshawe was employed against the Swedes on the Biorg and Viborg Sounds and was promoted to be Brigadier-General and received the Order of St. Vladimir 2nd grade in February 1793. In 1794 he served in Courland and Lithuania in the suppression of various Polish uprisings. On 1 March 1796 he was made Major-General by the Emperor Paul, in 1798 Lt. General and in February 1800, he attained the full rank of General. In September of the last year, he was appointed by the Emperor Alexander Inspector General of the Ukraine forces and Military Governor of Kieff, and in December 1803, Military Governor of Theodosia (Kaffa). There he remained several years and there his wife died on 6 September 1806 and was buried at Kertch. The cemetery is close to the sea.

In July 1807 he captured Anapa, for the second time from the Turks. The January of the next year, in consequence of the peace of Tilsit, he was at his own request, relieved of all military duties (5 July 1807) and remained in retirement for 4 years. His sister, Miss Althea Fanshawe records in her Diary that on several occasions during this period he desired that the Spanish & Portuguese papers of Viscount (Charles) Fanshawe might be sent to him.

In 1812 he was restored to his former military rank and served as a volunteer under the Duke of Wurtemburg at the siege of Danzig: but he was not again entrusted with any independent military command. A letter of his from Danzig dated January 1813, records that his son William was with him covered with decorations, that his son Frederick was A.D.C. to his father, and his son George, who had been wounded at Lutzen was A.D.C. to the Grand Duke Constantine.

In March 1816, he was granted in recognition of his long service, a fief of the village of Uleniee situated some 12 miles south of Warsaw and estimated to produce an income of about £900p.a. – and in the same month was appointed by Imperial decree a member of the Senate of Poland. During the summer Miss Fanshawe sent him by the hand of his son Frederick, the letters and papers of Sir Richard Fanshawe which had been at Shiplake and Bath. These and the above papers of Viscount Fanshawe have completely disappeared. It is believed that after the death of Frederick Fanshawe in 1831 they were conveyed to St. Petersburg and there utterly lost sight of.

In the summer of 1817 General Fanshawe came from St. Petersburg to Antwerp by sea with his son William and proceeded to Spa, where he was joined by his sister Mrs Jenkinson & her husband, and his own two sons, Henry & Charles Robert Fanshawe, the last of whom took his two eldest boys Charles Simon & John to see their grandfather. General Fanshawe did not re-visit England on this occasion; but after wintering in Ghent, returned in the early summer of 1818 to Russia where the last ten years of his life were spent, the summers at St. Petersburg or in its neighbourhood and the winters at Warsaw. In the autumn of 1825, he visited Teplitz and Carlsbad for his health, and twice in that year he mentioned his granddaughter Althea[1], who survived to 1916. Meanwhile his sons continued to serve and receive promotion, George being attached to the household of the Grand Duke Constantine.

The death of the Emperor Alexander I on 1 December 1825, and the resignation of the Grand Duke in favour of his younger brother, the Emperor Nicholas I, was regarded by the Fanshawes as a great blow to their fortunes. Constantine, however, was perfectly impossible as a ruler *(see the Cambridge Modern History Vo XV and the Encyclopedia Britannica upon him)* poccessing as he himself stated in his letter of resignation to his father "neither the courage nor capacity nor strength needed"; and even his resignation was mismanaged and led to outbreaks in a number of places, and to a very serious one in St. Petersburg where the Radicals stood for summoning a Diet to settle the question of

---

[1] Althea Hedwige Fanshawe (1825-1916) daughter of George Fanshawe, youngest son of Colonel Fanshawe - married her cousin Charles Alexander Fanshawe (2nd son of William Simon Fanshawe & Pauline Meisner).

succession, for reduction of army service and emancipation of the serfs. William and George Fanshawe were successful in keeping the troops they commanded loyal to the new Emperor, in spite of risings at Kieff and in various towns near Warsaw. General Fanshawe and his three sons made personal tender of their services to the new Czar, and in the spring of the year all proceeded to St. Petersburg, where the General sat on the High Court appointed in June to try the Decembrists without their being present. Of these, five were sentence to be hanged, 31 to be beheaded, and 85 to banishment to Siberia. General Fanshawe recorded his opinion that the punishments were not sufficiently severe. This was the last public service rendered by him.

Throughout the following year he was in very broken health, and postponed the visit of his eldest son from England, though he was able to express a wish to see the *MSS. Memoirs of Lady Fanshawe*, then under preparation for publication by Sir Harris Nicholas and on 4 August he signed, with a very shaky hand, a deed assigning his son Charles Robert a fifth of the sum of £12,000 settled on himself by Miss Anna Snelling.

On the 23rd February 1828 he died in Warsaw and was buried on the 27th, in the cemetery of the reformed church in that city with the honours due to his rank. By chance, the eldest grandson Charles Simon Faithfull Fanshawe happened to be at Warsaw with his uncles at the time. The three sons in Russia wrote on 5 March to the two sons in England informing them of all that had happened and stating that they were about to proceed to St. Petersburg to represent their claims to consideration in recognition of their father's services. Of these sons General William Fanshawe died within a year of his father on 17 February

1829 and Frederick Fanshawe died only two and a half years later, on 15 August 1831.

By his will executed on 19 January 1828, a month before his death, General Henry Fanshawe left all his real estate in England to his eldest son Henry, and his other property in that country equally to his four sons – excepting Charles Robert, who had already received his share. All his estate in Russia was left to the three sons in that country, and on his death, it was sold and the money divided. The will was attested by two brother Senators, and it was recorded that it was not in the handwriting of the General by reason of his weak state, which however did not affect his capacity for any judicial act. A picture of him in uniform, decorated with his various orders, is now [1927] in the possession of his great-granddaughter, Miss Caroline Fanshawe. He was knighted by the Emperor…"[1]

---

[1] An account of the lives of General Fanshawe's sons and their descendants follows in 'The History of the Fanshawe Family' - pages 287 – 319. (Available to view at Valence House Museum & Local Studies Centre, Dagenham, Essex or online - https://archive.org/details/historyoffanshaw00fans/page/n237/mode/2up).

Appendix 2

Caleb Hillier Parry
1755-1822

Caleb Hillier Parry was born in 1755 at Cirencester where he attended the same grammar school as his lifelong friend Edward Jenner[1]. After continuing his education at the Dissenters' Academy in Warrington he went to medical school in Edinburgh. Then studying a further two years with Dr Denman[2] of Middlesex Hospital, he returned to Edinburgh in 1777 to take his M.D in the subject of Rabies.

The following year, he married Sarah Rigby of Warrington, and they took an extended tour of Europe, before he set up practice at 13 Catherine Place, Bath.

The practice grew slowly - earning only £40 in the first year but then in 1785 when John Hunter[3] visited Bath and suffered from angina pectoris, Parry with Jenner (a former pupil of Hunter) had the care of that eminent doctor. This did much for Parry's reputation and his annual income soon rose to £1500 a year. Then, in a position to buy land near the edge of the city, he built up a flock of sheep as a hobby. This quickly developed into another absorbing scientific interest for as he observed the effects of crossbreeding Marino sheep with his English flock, he began a serious study of genetics.

At the same time, Parry and Jenner had set up the 'Fleece Medical Society' where at three meetings a year, the members were encouraged to present their specific medical

---

[1] Edward Jenner FRS FRCPE (1749 – 1823) physician and scientist who pioneered the concept of vaccines by creating the smallpox vaccine - the world's first vaccine.
[2] Thomas Denman M.D. (1733–1815) - a specialist in midwifery.
[3] (1728-1793) Leading Surgeon of the period, an early advocate for observation and scientific method in medicine.

interests and observations – often leading to publication of their work.

Always with that spirit of 'Enlightenment', the two friends constantly stimulated each other's interest in a wide range of subjects. Included was a shared youthful passion for fossil-hunting and 'Proposals for a History of the Fossils of Gloucestershire' was published by Parry in 1781. In 1807 Parry became a founder member of Bath's Geological Society.

Parry's imagination was also caught by the Montgolfier brothers when they launched the first hot air balloon in 1783. The following year, spectators gathered in Royal Crescent to see Parry successfully launch his own balloon, which he designed and created - including the apparatus to produce the hydrogen. The balloon flew for more than an hour and travelled nineteen miles.

Despite all these interests, none were at the expense of his medical career or his time for observations. His patients included many from the elite in art, science and politics, who attracted by his intelligent lively conversation, also became his friends.

However, Parry's primary interest remained in medicine and even when his career was advanced, he retained his staff appointments at Bath's General Hospital and the Casualty Hospital - often helping those most in need.

Much is written about Parry's character and whilst he clearly was an independent thinker and read extensively - the words charm and good looks, 'playfulness of manner' and a man full of amusing stories are those most often repeated. He seems to have been a most delightful friend to have had as a personal physician!

It also appears that this was not just an 'outside' face, as at home there were family musical evenings that were much enjoyed, where his pleasant singing voice was heard.

He had nine children, and the move in 1789 to Summerhill, a newly built house on the edge of the city, was intended to be a place with good air for them to grow – and it was there that he housed his vast library of medical books, today retained at Bristol University.

Parry's passion for medicine never wavered, and curiosity drove him to constantly enquire as to cause and effect of the human body. Consequently, when a patient died, he usually requested an autopsy and although he did not perform the procedure, he always attended at any hour of the night or day. He noted the condition of organs and learnt how the parts of the human form inter-acted together. His notes were extensive, and as he learnt and recorded, he was adding to medical knowledge for coming generations. His reputation became well known during his lifetime, but it was only after his death when his son Charles published his notes, that his real value came to be truly acknowledged.

Parry was the first to establish a relationship between angina and coronary heart disease and acknowledge that the functional efficiency of the coronary arteries was more indicative than their structural integrity. In his work on angina pectoris in 1799, he paid tribute to Jenner's observations. But Parry's treatment of angina was far ahead of his time – for he advised a simple diet with little fluid or fried, spicy foods, accompanied by gentle exercise.

In 1814 Parry published 'Cases of Tetanus & Rabies Contagiosa' which he dedicated to Edward Jenner. After having seen three cases of rabies in man, he was able to describe hydrophobia and give detailed descriptions of a patient and the subsequent necropsy. As prevention, he suggested a tax on dogs to decrease numbers; but such ideas were only acceptable to the public after Pasteur.

In 1816 Parry published 'The Nature, Cause and Varieties of the Arterial Pulse' - dedicated to Sir Joseph

Banks. Much of his experimentation for this was on animals, and his original observations on the human pulse are now generally accepted.

Although Parry's eldest son Charles was reluctant to study medicine[1] as his father wished, he did qualify as a doctor and after his father's death was able to put together his father's unpublished work. Proud of his father, he re-examined the notes to highlight his special findings - he mentions the descriptions of five cases of exophthalmic goitre - the first in 1786, when he noted enlargement of the jugular veins and other signs. This means that as Graves published in 1835, he added little to Parry's description and experts since have suggested Graves' Disease should be called Parry's Disease.

Parry also described idiopathic dilatation of the colon, known since 1887 as 'Hirschsprung's Disease', and that facial hemi atrophy, known as 'Romberg's Disease' (after the 19th century German physician), is now often named 'Romberg & Parry' as Caleb Parry described it in 1814.

Charles Parry notes from his own journal records, that when he personally suffered from asthma during the hay season, his father observed 'it was a seasonal affliction'.

In 1816, Caleb Hillier Parry's career was unfortunately cut short by a major stroke. With speech seriously affected and his right side paralysed, he survived six years with pain and great frustration. But his brain still functioned well, and he continued his research and was also able to find distraction by cataloguing his garden plants and trees, and dictating his memories to his daughter.

Parry was sixty-six when he died 9th March 1822. His friend Edward Jenner was a pallbearer at his funeral and said later: *'Poor Parry, I have just returned from Bath, where I*

---

[1] As a student he frustrated his father by taking a walking tour of the Harz Mountains in Germany, with his friend the poet Samual Taylor Coleridge.

went to attend his remains to the silent tomb. The manifestations of regard and affection exhibited by all ranks from Sion Hill to the Abbey bore unequivocal testimony to his worth and talents' – those remarks were confirmed by newspapers reports of streets lined with respectful crowds. After burial in Bath Abbey, a memorial tablet was raised on the south aisle, by his colleagues, the city's doctors.

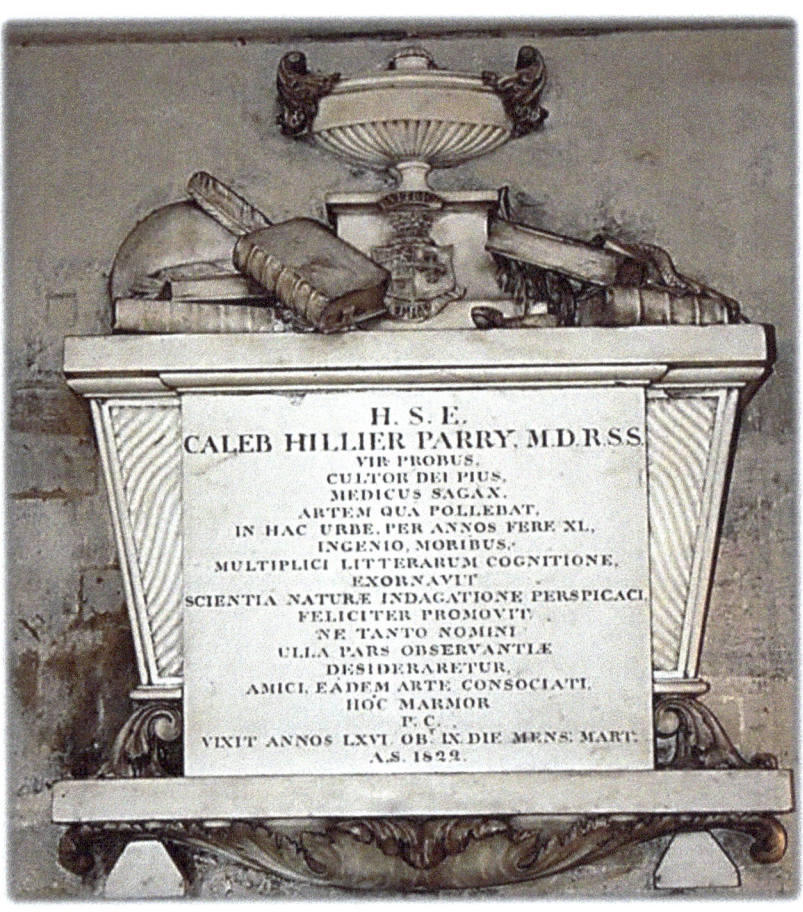

Practitioner's Medical Observations

Patient: Miss Althea Fanshawe

Extract

'Collections from the unpublished
medical writings of the late
Caleb Hillier Parry'

Contributors
Caleb Hillier Parry 1755-1822.
Charles Henry Parry 1779-1860.

St. Thomas's Hospital. Medical School. Library
King's College London
Publication: Underwoods, London 1825

https://wellcomecollection.org/works/zydfuzur

Various Remarks on Epilepsy, &c.—In Epilepsy and Hysteria there is a great impulse to make water. In the former also vomiting frequently, as also in apoplexy. But he who would therefore conclude that either disease depends on disorder of stomach, might as well infer that Epilepsy or Hysteria come from disease of the bladder or kidney.

In regard to *Epilepsy*, it will be well to inquire into the effects of impulse on the medulla oblongata, by the basilar artery. [1814.]

The beginning and end of each *epileptic fit*, before total insensibility begins, and after it ceases, is often delirium, screaming, false impressions, attempts to annoy others under these impressions, &c.

When Miss F. has what she calls an *attack*, which is short of an epileptic fit, the first symptom is a confusion in her head, which is always followed by an hysterical rising in her throat, and accompanied with incapacity of speaking and recollection.

Her pulse is seldom under 96 in a minute, and increases in frequency towards night, and always becomes quicker and quicker till the fit comes on, when, for two days, it is at the slowest, and other symptoms of disease the least. She has a great deal of the rumbling in the bowels, which is usually, though unjustly, attributed to wind.

Closing the lips and blowing out, as if in smoking, during sleep, accompanies certain states of *epileptic stupor;* and if occurring in a state of health, during sleep, is certainly an indication of a tendency to cerebral oppression.

A Modification of Nervous Affection.—Stammering.—In Miss F., as the cause of fits gradually accumulated during each interval, blood collected in the head, or continued to exhaust by stimulation, till convulsions produced a determination to the surface and extremities; stammering also began to occur with other symptoms, till relieved by a fit.

Effects of Stimuli.—In Miss F., a little eating and wine immediately takes off convulsions of the face, speechlessness, and very often pain of the head. Mr. C. says that it also makes the pulse slower. Great relief was in every respect obtained from Oleum Succini rectificatum, of which she took by degrees 114 drops twice a day in milk, two ounces.

How does this act? Surely by extending the determination, which did exist in the head, to the whole habit, and thus diminishing the former. It remains for me to prove that the stimulus may be partial; which I do by the circumstance of the head being unduly hot, while the feet are unduly cold. On leaving off Oleum Succini, though it was rather gradually decreased, the fits and attacks were amazingly increased, and the indisposition during the intervals much aggravated. By degrees, under the use of Ether, health became as usual.

upwards of twenty years afterwards, had no return of that malady.

Epileptic Attacks.—Miss F. has been subject to epileptic fits for many years, and to a minor paroxysm, which she calls attacks, to which she was liable from the very beginning of her illness, though she kept no account of them for the first six years. The following is a list of these different states, the last of which sometimes occurred as often as three times a day. From September, when first taken with a fit, in the year

			Attacks
1794 she had	11 Fits		
1795	41		
1796	38		
1797	37		
1798	42		
1799	37		
1800	40		145
1801	32		75
1802	41		194
1803	27		25
1804	29		61
1805	29		128
1806	29		158
1807	29		130
1808	26		144
1809	22		175
1810	26		233
1811	26		128
1812	31		152
	593		1743

Epilepsy. 421

It may be added, that this lady continued to suffer in the same manner till her death, which happened in 1823. During this whole period, Miss F. had devoted herself much to reading and writing, and had been the esteemed authoress of several volumes. (E.)

Appendix 3

From Manuscript to Print - 1829

The Memoirs
of
Ann, Lady Fanshawe (LDVAL8

With a dedication by Revd Charles Fanshawe to his patron:
Princess Adelaide, Duchess of Clarence,
Queen Consort of King William VI

The Memoirs of Ann, Lady Fanshawe

The Fanshawe family story is full of insightful glimpses into the lives and characters of many interesting personalities, but none has captured the public's imagination as much as that of Ann, Lady Fanshawe and her husband Sir Richard Fanshawe.

Their story, charged with romance and action, traces their meeting during the English Civil War while at the court in exile at Oxford and follows their lives together as they experience great personal triumph along with the deepest sorrow. As Royalists close to King Charles I, they were with him through his many vicissitudes, and never waiving in their support, shared many hazardous adventures. Then when safety was at stake for Charles, Prince of Wales, heir to the throne, it was their responsibility to convey him safely into exile at the court of France.

After the Restoration, when Sir Richard Fanshawe was appointed Charles II's first ambassador to Portugal and Spain, the couple rode into Madrid in magnificent procession. But such happiness was short-lived, as Ann Fanshawe, so stoic in suffering the loss of many children and having overcome enormous difficulties throughout marriage; found herself helpless when her husband was suddenly struck down with a fever. After his death, undeterred by the difficulties, Lady Ann accompanied by her husband's ambassadorial entourage, brought his body across Spain and France for burial with his family at Ware.

This 17th century story of love and fortitude through war and conflict, was recounted by Ann Fanshawe in her memoirs written in 1676. That manuscript was intended for their only surviving son Richard[1] to learn the story of the father he would never know and was not intended for publication. However, when that second Sir Richard Fanshawe died unmarried in 1694, the manuscript remained within his family passing through succeeding generations of his sister Ann Fanshawe, born 1654/5.

That situation is explained in this extract from HFF...'
An old memorandum at Parsloes states that she married Mr Ryder, and her uncle Sir Edmund Turnor mentions her as "Ann Ryder Fanshawe, alias Ryder" in his will (1704), but the date of her marriage is not ascertained. It must, however, have taken place between 28 May 1680 - when her signature appears on a release to her sister Katherine[2]– and 1685, when her daughter Ann Ryder was born: the latter being said to be of the age of 14 at the time when her marriage licence with "John Lawrence of Westminster, gent" was granted in 1699. "Ann Lawrence, daughter of niece Ryder" was left a legacy under the will of Sir Edmund Turnor. It is supposed that Lady Fanshawe's great grand-daughter Charlotte Coleman, whose will dated 6 September 1766, and proved in 1768, was the daughter of Ann Lawrence. The edition of Lady Fanshawe's Memoirs published in 1829 was taken from a copy of the transcript made by Charlotte Coleman in 1766.'...

Ann, Lady Fanshawe & Sir Richard Fanshawe
|
Ann Fanshawe (born 1654/5) m Mr Ryder
|
Ann Ryder (born 1685) m John Lawrence of Westminster
(married 1699)
|
Charlotte Lawrence (d. 1768) m Coleman

---

[1] Sir Richard Fanshawe 2nd Baronet died unmarried 1694.
[2] Katherine Fanshawe died unmarried 1719.

Late in the 19th century, the original manuscript was passed down to Evelyn Fanshawe of Parsloes, whereupon his distant cousin Herbert C Fanshawe then produced 'The Memoirs of Ann, Lady Fanshawe 1600-1672' - published by John Lane Co. This transcription is generally considered the most accurate of all those published and also includes nearly 400 pages of comprehensive notes.

Nevertheless, credit for the initiative of bringing the memoirs first to publication remains with Revd Charles Fanshawe for his edition of 1829. Therefore, in consequence of his close connection to Althea Fanshawe, it is of interest to follow the events which made that possible.

A comment in the HFF is interesting as it relates to the year 1827 and the Revd Fanshawe's father, General Henry Fanshawe[1] of the Russian Army: *'Throughout the following year he* [the General] *was in very broken health and postponed the visit of his eldest son* [Henry] *from England, though he was able to express a wish to see the MSS Memoirs of Lady Fanshawe, then under preparation for publication by Sir Harris Nicholas'*…

The publication being prepared was from a 'copy' of the original manuscript, as clarified in this extract from the Notes included in HCF's own later publication of the Memoirs…*'various copies of the MSS exist in the family, all derived from this* [the original] *or possibly from other originals contemporary with this. In one of these copies owned at present by Mrs Jebb,* [granddaughter of General Jenkinson, to whom Frances Fanshawe, daughter of Simon Fanshawe [the head of the family in his day, who died in 1777), was married] *- are notes which trace the MSS from the original, through a copy in 1766 by Lady*

---

[1] General Fanshawe died on 23rd February 1828 in Warsaw.

Fanshawe's great-granddaughter Charlotte Coleman and Mrs Bell Chauncey. The former left the copy to Mr E.S Bowdler[1] and from it Miss Althea Fanshawe (daughter of Simon Fanshawe and sister of Frances Jenkinson) transcribed a copy in 1786. This copy is however made on paper with the watermark of 1796 and is therefore clearly one from that of Miss Althea Fanshawe. As she left all her property to her nephew, the Reverend Charles Robert Fanshawe, the dedicator of the first printed editions of the memoirs, it would seem almost certain that her copy was the text used for these.

A second copy of her transcript, owned by the late Admiral Sir Edward Fanshawe GCB, contains the endorsement, "Transcribed in the year 1766 by her great-granddaughter Charlotte Coleman. This lady died in 1768 and left this manuscript, copied by her own hand and that of her friend Mrs Bell Chauncey to E S Bowdler."

"Transcribed in the year 1786 from the MSS lent me by Mrs Bowdler". (signature) *"Althea Fanshawe."*

"Neither the copy of Miss A Fanshawe nor the original copy of the MSS made by Miss Charlotte Coleman is now forthcoming."

Original death records for Bath confirm 'Charlotte Coleman, gentlewoman' died 19th August 1768 and if as previously maintained, the lady left no heirs, she would have been the last of the line of Sir Richard & Ann Fanshawe.

Keeping that in mind, we must now establish a link between Charlotte Coleman and the Bowdler family if we are to explain why they had possession of the copy manuscript.

---

[1] HCF is in error as E S Bowdler is Mrs Elizabeth Stuart Bowdler, daughter of Sir John Cotton of Connington and mother of Henrietta Bowdler, the close friend of Althea Fanshawe.

Firstly, we should note here that contrary to previous thought, the friendship between Althea Fanshawe and Henrietta Bowdler must have predated Althea's permanent removal to Bath in 1803. This is confirmed by the fact that the manuscript used for the 1829 publication was one made available by the Bowdler family to be copied by Althea Fanshawe some years before the end of the 18th century.

We must then note that when HCF researched the various owners of the manuscripts, he confirmed Charlotte Coleman died in 1768. He also indicated that the 'copy' manuscript was copied by Charlotte Coleman's hand together with that of her friend Mrs Bell Chauncey, before it was later passed to [Mrs] E.S Bowdler. However, is it not curious that he makes no attempt to explain any connection between the three individuals?

Today, with the advantage of exploring public family records electronically, it has now been possible to offer a logical link between the three ladies.

If we presume that when preparing The Memoirs and the HFF, the author did not delve with any detail into Althea's interest in writing, religion and women's education, we may conclude that he did not discover that those were the interests she shared with a coterie of women who surrounded her. As a result, he probably did not appreciate the manuscript had been passed to Mrs Elizabeth Stuart Bowdler[1] and not Mr E S Bowdler. With that information, he may have discovered that her unexplained friend *'Bell*

---

[1] Mrs Elizabeth Stuart Bowdler of Box, near Bath was a writer with a particular interest in the advancement of education, often mentioned along with Mrs Trimmer. As a member of the high church movement of the Church of England, to a greater or lesser degree, all her children followed her interests and centred their writing upon church and education.

Chauncey' was possibly a person who might provide a distant familial link to Charlotte Coleman and the Fanshawe family!

Isabella Chauncy was a spinster daughter of Dr Chauncy of Derby. One of her sisters, Frances was the wife of Dr Thomas Lawrence[1] of Westminster. From public record we know that 'Bell' died in 1787 and through her extensive will the names of all her Lawrence nephews and nieces are provided. Immediately after their bequests, appear the names of the three daughters of Thomas & Elizabeth Stuart Bowdler of Bath – Jane, Frances & Henrietta Maria, who each received five guineas for a ring.

Establishing a close friendship between Bell Chauncy and Elizabeth Stuart Bowdler was obviously not surprising, but the name of Lawrence as a brother-in-law of Isabella Chauncy might indicate a possible connection to Charlotte Coleman. So, the outstanding question remains of establishing a link between this Lawrence family and Charlotte Coleman's grandfather – John Lawrence of Westminster who married Ann Ryder in 1699.

Unfortunately, at present that has not been possible. Available are extensive biographical details of Dr Thomas Lawrence who we learn was the son of Captain Thomas Lawrence and there was another son, who although mentioned is unnamed. Then, the doctor had a great uncle, Dr Henry Lawrence who was physician to Queen Anne – but records show no mention of a family. Clearly the 'Lawrence' family were long established in Westminster, so it can only be assumed that 'John Lawrence of Westminster', the father

---

[1] President of the Royal College of Physicians and close friend of Dr Samuel Johnson.

of Charlotte Coleman, gentlewoman – probably was connected to this family.

Even if Charlotte Coleman died without any known direct relatives, it is difficult to imagine she would have left the manuscript of Ann, Lady Fanshawe with complete strangers. If she and Isabella were distantly related, is it not more possible they were together to make the copy knowing their relationship, than just the coincidence of names? We know Charlotte and Bell died within a year of each other, and as a mutual friend, Elizabeth Stuart Bowdler probably was trusted with the manuscript, receiving it from Bell for onward transmission to the Fanshawe family.

The gentry knew well their family connections and generally moving within well-formed circles, many marriages were contracted through these networks. Just as the children of Mrs Bowdler were close to Althea and her family; so too were the families of Chauncy & Bowdler. Eventually, Bell's niece Elizabeth Lawrence became the second wife of a George Gipps, and when her stepson George married, his bride was Jane Bowdler – Henrietta Bowdler's niece.

But the subject of marriage was not one that seemed to have enthused Althea and Henrietta, as both since their youth had ambitions of writing and publishing. In the 18th century, many ladies successfully earned their living through their ability to write, and all well understood that such opportunities only came through education.

It is not coincidental that Althea notes in her diary the activities of many ladies who aspired to educate women. Although she had independent means, she admired others who lived by their pen and the Age of Enlightenment could not have illuded Althea…

Was it Ann Fanshawe's ability to rise above misfortune with fortitude that intrigued Althea and her friends? Did they also recognise her clever and intelligent use of female guile? They knew the Civil War had advanced women's lives, so did they also recognise that changes were being brought by the Napoleonic wars?

With wit and comedy in her writing, it is curious that Althea did not attempt a novel. Perhaps the answer lies within the interesting theory posed by the Australian feminist writer Dale Spender who during the great feminist movement of the 1980's wrote an insightful book called 'Mothers of the Novel'[1].

She revealed that there were many women novelists who wrote well and had successfully published to critical acclaim, prior to the period of Jane Austin. Then, in the early 19th century the reputations of all those ladies were sacrificed to allow male writers to be promoted, leaving us with the impression that it was Austen who invented the female novel!

Do any of these feminist ideas relate to Althea Fanshawe or even Ann, Lady Fanshawe? Interestingly for Dale Spender they do - as she proposes that Ann Fanshawe was one of four[2] 17th century women who were responsible for launching new literary traditions. She states that by blurring fact and fiction, each provides us with the beginnings of the modern novel – *"What can be said with certainty is that she [Ann Fanshawe] wrote with sensitivity and skill, that she wrote a good story which sustained the interest of the reader, and which was most convincing and entertaining. In the end it doesn't matter just how true or objective her account was.*

---

[1] Dale Spender (1943-2023) published by Pandora Press in 1986.
[2] Anne Clifford, Lucy Hutchinson, Anne Fanshawe & Margaret Cavendish.

What matters is that her 'Memoirs' are one of the early models of good women's writing".

How fascinating that Ann Fanshawe's story endures to be compared with all the key elements of modern fiction but undoubtely, her story continues to be enjoyed by women of all generations who understand love, loss and loyalty.

Perhaps too, in this age of equality, we should acknowledge that those enduring qualities are also often appreciated by sensitive men - so might we include Revd Charles Fanshawe?

Althea's diary leaves the impression of Revd Charles being a rather selfish young man, but life events, including the loss of his young wife, may have taught him sensitivity. If that were so, perhaps as Chaplain to Adelaide, Duchess of Clarence, Charles Fanshawe saw Ann Fanshawe's story with the tragic loss of children, in parallel with the fate of his Patroness – and caused him to offer his dedication to the Duchess, in that first publication?

This theory may only be based on coincidence, but nevertheless we must hope that Adelaide, the future Queen Consort of England received from her Chaplain, kindly sympathy accompanied by wise counsel.

Illustrations & Acknowledgments

The majority of images included were sourced via Wikimedia Commons and classified as within the public domain. The exceptions are listed below.

Hopefully all sources are included but in view of the wide use of many of the images over many years, copyright it is not always apparent. If we have omitted or failed to obtain prior permission our sincere apologies are offered in advance.

Althea Fanshawe Bookplate and diary images	Valence House Museum
William Fanshawe of Parsloes (1583 – 1634)	Valence House Museum
Simon Fanshawe of Fanshawe Gate	Valence House Museum
Caroline of Brunswick, Princess of Wales	V&A Museum
Hatchard's Logo	Hartchard's Website
Sir Robert Stopford	National Maritime Museum
Thomas Dimsdale	NPG – Public Domain
Charles Fanshawe	Valence House Museum
The Signing of the Treaty of Ghent	Smithsonion Museum
Captain Robert Fanshawe RN	Valence House Museum
Scene in Plymouth Sound 1815	National Maritime Museum
Sir Richard Fanshawe	Valence House Museum
John Fanshawe of Shabden	Fanshawe Private Collection
Hannah More	NPG – Public Domain
George Hyde Wollaston	NPG – Public Domain

Princess Charlotte of Wales	Museum of NZ - Public Domain
Duchess of Kent	Royal Coll. of Belgium Public Domain
John Eardley Wilmot	Yale Center for Brit. Art - Public Domain
Right Hon. George Canning, MP	National Trust Collection - Public Domain
Ann, Lady Fanshawe	Valence House Museum
Princess Adelaide, Duchess of Clarence	Royal Collection – Wikicommons

Historical Resources for Further Reading

There are endless resources available, here are just a few.

Many of these books of references are out of print and only available online or in reprinted editions through online booksellers. There are later books available on this subject, but these older publications were among those that helped to establish an authentic tone to the thoughts of Althea when transcribing her diary.

'A Testimony of Her Times' by Sarah Markham - based on Penelope Hind's Diaries and Correspondence 1787-1838.

'Revd Charles Phillott' - https://www.badseysociety.uk/1661-1996-vicars-badsey-aldington-and-wickhamford-plurality/1807-1851-reverend-charles-phillott

'Thoughts on Affection: addressed chiefly to young people' – Althea Fanshawe (1805)
Published by Richard Cruttwell, St James Street, Bath.

'Henry Fanshawe RN'
https://historyinportsmouth.co.uk/events/hero.html reprint: HardPress (2019) ISBN 9780371671269

'King George III' – John Brooke (1972) – Granada Press

'Mothers of the Novel' – Dale Spender (1986) – Pandora

'The History of the Fanshawe Family' – H C Fanshawe (1927) Andrew Reid & Co.

'The Memoirs of Ann, Lady Fanshawe'

'Charlotte & Leopold'
James Chambers (2007) Old Street Publishing

'Passages from the Diaries of Mrs Philip Lybbe Powys of Hardwick House 1756-1808'
Edited by Emily J Climenson (1899) – Reprint available

'The Journal of Mrs Elizabeth Hall of Harpsden Court (1800 – 1804)' available to download online.

The Archives & Local Studies Centre at Valence House, has for many years been the hub of historical research for the London Borough of Barking & Dagenham and among the vast archives is 'The Fanshawe Collection' relating to the Fanshawe family resident in the borough from Tudor times.

Year on year Fanshawe family members continue to deposit their documents and papers allowing the staff & research volunteers to make new discoveries. Each generation with a different story to tell helps to build a picture that reflects the history of our nation.

Currently, the volunteer Fanshawe researchers Deirdre Marculescu, Rosalind Alexander and Lorna Orr are slowly working to bring the lives of the late 18th and 19th centuries to public attention and they are helped by Derek Alexander, Valence volunteer computer expert. The legacy from our 2016 grant from the Heritage Lottery still makes this possible along with encouragement from Valence staff and fellow volunteers. Most of all, we are inspired by the interest and enthusiasm of the Fanshawe family for sharing their family treasures so that as historical resources they will be used and enjoyed by a wider audience.

www.ingramcontent.com/pod-product-compliance
Lightning Source LLC
Chambersburg PA
CBHW041136110526
44590CB00027B/4036